Addiction and Pastoral Care

NICHOLAS ROBERTS

Addiction and Pastoral Care

CANTERBURY
PRESS
Norwich

© Nicholas Roberts 2018

First published in 2018 by the Canterbury Press Norwich
Editorial office
3rd Floor, Invicta House
108–114 Golden Lane
London EC1Y OTG, UK
www.canterburypress.co.uk

Canterbury Press is an imprint of Hymns Ancient & Modern Ltd
(a registered charity)

Ancient
&Modern

Hymns Ancient & Modern® is a registered trademark of
Hymns Ancient & Modern Ltd
13A Hellesdon Park Road, Norwich,
Norfolk NR6 5DR, UK

British Library Cataloguing in Publication data

A catalogue record for this book is available
from the British Library

978 1 84825 974 4

Typeset by Regent Typesetting
Printed and bound in Great Britain by
CPI Group (UK) Ltd, Croydon

Contents

Acknowledgements

I wish to extend my thanks to many people who have kindly contributed their knowledge, experience and professional expertise to the preparation of this book, and in particular:

Dr David Ball

Reverend Leo Booth

Professor Luke Bretherton

Ms Diana Howard

Professor Alister McGrath

Professor Michael Holwill

The staff of Hymns Ancient and Modern, particularly Christine Smith

I also wish to pay tribute to the pioneering work of the late Father Kenneth Leech.

The book is dedicated to all who have suffered from alcohol or drug dependency, and all those who work to try to understand and help them.

Introduction

The Need for this Book on Addiction and Pastoral Care

The purpose of this book is to provide a practical guide to the pastoral care of people who are substance dependent, that is to say, addicted to the use of alcohol or illicit drugs such as heroin, or in some cases both. I hope that it will enable ministers of many Christian denominations, including lay pastors, to minister in a way that is both knowledgeable and confident to substance misusers and their families, whether in parish ministry or in other contexts, such as hospital, university, or prison chaplaincy. I present a pastoral model that I have devised, which I call my 'aspirational model', based on a positive understanding of human desires and goals for living well. I give this model a solid basis in both theological and psychological terms.

My professional background consists mainly of my work as an Anglican chaplain in the NHS for over 20 years, which has shaped my reflections on encounters in hospitals with addicted individuals. I have also experienced addiction among my own family and friends. I have studied the subject at academic level at King's College London and the Institute of Psychiatry in south London, and in recent years have led training courses for ministers on addiction ministry in three Anglican dioceses in the London area.

Some time ago I went to visit a college friend who, like me, was ordained as a Church of England priest. He had had problems in a previous parish in the south of England, and I knew that he had been drinking heavily at times; but he seemed settled in his present job, and I genuinely thought that things had settled down and that he was doing well again. When we spoke on the telephone a few days before my visit he told me that he had bought a new car, and would meet me at his local railway station. We met as arranged, and I admired his gleaming new car. Then a few weeks later he called me to say that he had been driving down his local high street after drinking too much and had crashed his car, writing it off, although he had not been badly hurt. What followed this incident was a sudden (Damascus road) moment of realization that he needed help – a decision he had been avoiding for at least ten years!

It is now over 30 years since that 'moment', as my friend describes it. After going through an intensive detox, he continues to attend Alcoholics Anonymous meetings. I have twice attended AA meetings with him as a personal guest and observer. I have often referred to his recovery from alcoholism as *resurrection*. His story appears in a number of books that have been published since he began his recovery from addiction: *Spirituality and Recovery* has a chapter that describes that accident and its consequences.[1] A drawing of him sitting on the kerb, head in hands, beside his wrecked car, makes the point far more vividly than his words. However, he has some-

---

1 Leo Booth, *Spirituality and Recovery* – a classic introduction to the difference between spirituality and religion in the process of healing. See chapter 4, 'My Moment' in particular.

times been criticized for talking about his personal experience in sermons in church – as if addiction is so shameful that it can't be mentioned in a sermon!

The inspirational story of his recovery from alcoholism has encouraged me to write this book, setting out some theoretical ideas and elements of discussion of addiction issues. It also tells the story of real human beings I have known personally, whose battle with addiction has been part of my life too, as I have tried to provide support and companionship to them – and in some cases their families – over many years. I have sometimes felt much frustration about knowing how best to help them, and it can be a long, uphill battle with many false starts and setbacks along the road to recovery.

I mention this at the outset because I know from experience that it is tempting to feel that we have failed as pastors when the people we are trying to help find the long road to sobriety very difficult and long-winded, and yet that is true for so many people. 'Cunning, powerful and baffling' is an expression that Alcoholics Anonymous sometimes uses to describe the experience of alcohol dependency. But this book also makes the important point that for many, perhaps most, people with addictions of one kind or another, there can be a way out of that particular form of slavery to substances and behaviours that diminish an individual's potential for a happy, rewarding and fulfilling life. *There is always room for hope that with the right treatment these addictions can be overcome.* I also encourage us never to see addicted people as 'them' or 'others' as if we were perhaps superior to those with obvious substance use disorders, such as the heroin addict. Gerald May's groundbreaking book *Addiction and Grace* invites us to see that we *all* stand in danger of becoming addicted, even to arguably good things like hard work and the desire for a reasonable amount of success and recognition in our work and personal relationships.

A further hope for this book originated in an encounter with a young man with a long history of substance misuse who was finding it very hard even in a well-regarded rehab unit to make any progress. One day I asked him a simple – perhaps rather naive – question: 'What do you want out of life?' Many months later, when he was much better and getting ready to move out of the residential treatment centre, he told me spontaneously that my question had triggered his recovery in a way that nothing else had up to that point.

That made me wonder what it was about my question that had been a turning point for him. And if it could be for him, might it not potentially be for others? In this book I suggest that this approach could be adopted more widely, certainly in our shared pastoral ministry, but also perhaps in clinical settings in the community.

My model for pastoral engagement with people with addiction problems – my 'aspirational model' – differs significantly from the traditional medical model by *beginning in a new place*. Instead of starting by looking at what has caused the addiction, I focus on *positive things*, the desires, longings and aspirations of the addicted person, and try to find ways of working with each person as a unique individual so that at least some of these might be achievable. This approach concentrates on the *person* rather than the *problem*, and helps the substance-dependent person to begin to take responsibility for making new plans for the future. This is not to suggest that questions about the reasons for the addiction should be ignored, but they are moved to a place of secondary rather than primary importance.

That brings me on to one of the most important contributions this book offers to those who are endeavouring to help people who are addicted to drugs or other substances. It provides theoretical but also practical guidance to Christian pastors who are professionally engaged with the addicted person. My aim is to shine some theological light on the subject of addiction, in terms of the relationship between sickness and sinfulness, and what the Christian tradition understands about human desires, longing and aspirations. How do our human desires find a legitimate home within the life of a Christian worshipping community?

The main purpose of this book is to help Christian pastors involved in the care of people who are addicted to alcohol or illicit drugs such as heroin. There are, of course, other kinds of addiction, such as addiction to gambling, but my focus is on substance addiction, recognizing that there are common factors in all addictions: in particular there is the aim of finding a short cut to excitement or to the relief of emotional pain and suffering. I hope this book will give both information about many aspects of the study of addiction and *practical guidance* to help us provide professional pastoral care that is well-informed and confident. It works from two specific theoretical and practical foundations, those of theology and psychology, in the belief that these two approaches together can be of considerable help in understanding what is going on and how we can respond positively and safely when we are faced with difficult individual and family issues around drugs and alcohol. Addiction is one area of healthcare in which the NHS could work collaboratively with well-informed pastoral care for the benefit of people who are suffering from addiction, and of course for their families as well.

The possibility of this kind of collaboration was recognized by Stephen Hales (1677–1761), a Church of England clergyman who achieved distinction in the medical sciences and was awarded a Fellowship of the Royal Society. One of the subjects he studied was alcohol misuse. He monitored the effects of alcohol on his parishioners, both from a medical point of view with his detailed clinical knowledge about the damage caused to the human body by excessive alcohol consumption, and in terms of the spiritual and ethical problems associated with excessive alcohol consumption, which had not decreased in the UK following the Gin Act of 1729. This Act of Parliament imposed a £20 licence fee on all gin retailers, but did nothing to reduce consumption of the beverage.[2] Hales' book *A Friendly Admonition* – cautioning against the misuse of alcohol on

---

2 The consumption of gin in 1729 is reckoned to have probably been in excess of a pint a week for every woman, child or man. See James Nicholls, *The Politics of Alcohol*, chapter 3.

physiological, theological and ethical grounds – was published by the Society for the Promotion of Christian Knowledge, and distributed to gaols, hospitals and the homes of his own parishioners.

So, approaching the topic from both disciplines in alliance is the methodology of this book, looking to find a way of integrating *scientific* (essentially psychological) and *theological* views of the subject of substance dependency and addiction as Hales discusses in his book.

On this basis the questions addressed in this book include:

- How can I safely help people as a pastor without getting into areas that are beyond my knowledge and competence?
- What kinds of treatment are available for people with addiction problems? What help is there for their children and partners?
- How can I easily access these treatments for someone who needs them? And where can I get support in trying to provide professionally competent help myself – for example, through locally based training courses?

Some of this ground is covered here as an introduction to the subject. Above all, I hope that the book will be a practical reference manual to help you keep in mind some of the important questions I have encountered in the course of the training sessions I have led and discussed with a wide range of Christian pastors working in parishes and other forms of ministry.

So, substance misuse is the specific focus of this book, with detailed insight into what causes addiction and how it can be treated successfully. An understanding of how pastoral ministry can be offered to addicted people and their families is provided, remembering that it is not only the individuals who misuse substances who need help, because their networks of family, professional and social relationships also suffer as a direct result of the addiction. As Marina Barnard says in her book *Drug Addiction and Families*, we should not underestimate the sense of shock that many families feel when they first discover that a family member is misusing a drug. This shock has many dimensions including dismay and sadness, and may involve the anger that comes from a sense of being let down by that person. Family members may also feel that they have somehow let the addicted person down by not recognizing the reality of that addiction or not knowing how to help. And the process by which that individual will be enabled to move out of the slavery of addiction to a new and fulfilling life within the family and society may well be long and hard. It is often the case that people who misuse drugs need to go into treatment more than once.

But we should also take account of Kenneth Leech's view in his book *Drugs and Pastoral Care*, where he argues that there is really no such thing as a specific ministry to addicts, partly because that risks labelling them: in a way, that can be an abuse of power. Leech even rejects the use of the word 'client' in the treatment of addicted people; he believed that labelling people 'does not fit well with the Christian view of what it is to be human, or with the doctrine of the Body of Christ in which all are equal'.[3]

---

3 Kenneth Leech, *Drugs and Pastoral Care*, p. 100.

What is Addiction? The World of Drugs and Alcohol

Drugs are rarely out of the news. Apart from TV and newspaper accounts of things like binge drinking in relation to alcohol, we know that there is much misuse of both prescription and non-prescription drugs in our society today. We are familiar with names like cannabis, heroin or crack cocaine, which have been around for many years. Their procurement, or obtaining the money needed for this, is likely to involve crime, which is often violent. It is likely that the majority of people currently in prison for violent behaviour have been involved in the production and distribution of illicit drugs. New drugs come on to the market with increasing frequency, sometimes referred to (no doubt inaccurately) as 'legal highs', or party drugs: these are definitely not safe substances that can be used without the possibility of harm to the user. Recently the use of 'spice' has become problematic: in Manchester some people have been reduced, at least temporarily, to what has been described as a 'zombie-like state'. Others have been paralysed, and this dangerous substance can cause serious cardiac and psychological problems. There has been violence and disruption through its use, particularly in prisons.

In response to the growing availability and use of these 'legal highs' the UK government introduced the Psychoactive Substances Act in 2016, but this has been challenged in the courts and its effectiveness is under scrutiny at the time of writing. Young people especially seem to be unaware of the serious long-term health risks of these substances which are readily available in pubs and nightclubs. Use of these substances is widespread in prisons where, as we have seen on the news, drones can be used to get them into the cells.

It was estimated in 2017[1] that in excess of 200,000 people worldwide are dying each year as a result of drug overdose and other related conditions such as HIV. In the USA, to give one example, 91 people per day die from opioid overdoses. On alcohol statistics, 3.3 million people worldwide die from alcohol-related conditions every year. And recent UK statistics tell us that in general 15 per cent of attendances at hospital casualty departments are directly linked to excessive alcohol consumption, a figure that rises to 70 per cent at weekends. This is by any standards alarming reading, particularly as we recognize the strain that A&E departments experience on their resources. And this is one good reason for looking at the situation and its causes, and thinking about what kind of help people should be getting to conquer their addictions, including the pastoral care offered by Christian ministers both in parishes and in other places where they work, including prisons.

As pastors it is likely that we will have met people who are using drugs, or know of family members who are at risk. We need to think how we might respond to their situation, particularly when an individual can be described as addicted to a substance such as heroin.

The first thing we need to do is learn something about the drug scene, and also about how to distinguish what might be considered normal use of alcohol, for example, from dependent or addictive use of alcohol, and a variety of other substances.

So in order to think in a systematic way about addiction in general, and particularly when it takes the form of dependence on such substances as alcohol, heroin or cocaine, we need to know how to *define what we mean by addiction*. Most of us know people who drink alcohol on a regular basis, but it would be odd to suggest that all use of alcohol is necessarily problematic. Some healthcare psychologists deny that addiction exists

---

1 This information comes from a *National Geographic* magazine article published in September 2017.

at all, although they represent one end of a spectrum of thinking on the subject, and many would disagree. But the widely held view is that some people do become addicted either to substances (such as alcohol) or activities (such as gambling), and that such addictions are best thought of as symptoms of a disease that in many cases will require some form of clinical treatment.

So what distinguishes normal enjoyment of such things from what may be regarded as pathological behaviour? A simple definition of addiction is offered by Professor Robert West of London University: addiction 'is a syndrome in which a reward seeking behaviour has become out of control'.[2]

The American Psychiatric Association's Diagnostic manual (DSM-V, 2013) and the World Health Organization's International Classification of Diseases (1992) are useful in this context, both focusing on an excessive desire for the consumption of a variety of drugs and difficulties in giving up their use. In particular they recognize the diagnostic importance of *tolerance* – the need for constantly increasing amounts of the drug to achieve the same effect, and *withdrawal symptoms* when the drug is not available, or the use of the drug to relieve the symptoms that occur when the effect of the drug has worn off (the 'morning after' drink for the alcoholic, for example).

It is not easy to be precise about when a substance user has become substance dependent. In the UK, various governments have tried to provide guidelines about the number of units of alcohol that an individual can safely drink on a weekly basis.[3] These numbers are revised, usually downwards, from time to time. A 70 cl bottle of whisky contains around 28 units of alcohol, and a 70 cl bottle of table wine usually somewhere between 9 and 12 units. People who frequently exceed these weekly amounts are at risk of addiction, and anyone regularly consuming a bottle of whisky or more on a daily basis, or its

---

2 Robert West, *Theory of Addiction*, p. 10. He also refers on page 15 to these two classification systems.

3 It may, however, be dangerous to consume all the allowed units in two days rather than spread them out over several days or a week.

equivalent, is almost certainly an alcoholic. With illicit drugs the tolerance and withdrawal factors can be used as a gauge to calculate the degree of dependency on a case-by-case basis.

Looking at the reasons why people become addicted to alcohol and/or drugs, a number of factors need to be considered. From a scientific perspective, it is becoming widely accepted that there is a *genetic* element in addiction, and well-regarded biological studies in alcohol dependency in particular have shown that certain genetic profiles play a significant part in the development of an addiction. That must not be taken to mean that genes 'cause' addiction in a direct way, but they can *predispose an individual to become substance dependent* if the circumstances of his life provide further impetus in that direction. So we can talk realistically about an *inherited vulnerability to substance dependency* that affects some people.

Other factors may well contribute towards substance dependency. First, there is the mysterious and sometimes baffling nature of addiction. There is no universal reason why people become addicted, although it is easy – if usually unhelpful – to attribute its origins to weakness of the will or sinfulness. There may be as many reasons for addiction as there are addicted people – a view that does not make the pastoral task any easier, but is at least realistic. Those who have worked with addicted individuals will perhaps recognize this feeling of bafflement about the situation. It can be very hard to understand why someone becomes substance dependent when the circumstances of his life seem, superficially at least, to be positive and rewarding; or why after successful treatment for the addiction the individual reverts to substance-dependent living, which unfortunately occurs in many cases.

There are widely recognized pathways, however. One is the 'chasing the dragon' factor, the desire for the buzz that can come from the use of alcohol and other drugs such as heroin or ecstasy. Some writers have drawn a comparison between this and the excitement of sexual activity. The use of amphetamines (speed) first became well known in the UK in the 1960s, when this form of drug use started to be recognized in the news media, and the term 'purple hearts', a combination of amphetamine and barbiturate, often associated with young people in the entertainment industry, became familiar.

Second, in some social groups (perhaps particularly among young people) there can be peer pressure to engage in drug use, which can easily get out of control. There is here a 'mimetic' element, when people adopt the lifestyle of a particular social group without perhaps taking account of their own genuine personal wishes and needs. We should also take into account the availability, affordability and social acceptability of some substance use, particularly alcohol.

Third, people use drugs to try to combat negative or painful psychological experiences, such as depression or anxiety. These may, of course, be symptomatic of a possibly serious or long-term mental disturbance that could be better treated by proper clinical intervention; non-prescription drugs may well make the situation worse. Addiction can also be triggered by a difficult period in a person's life, perhaps involving one or more major life-changing events – such as excessive stress, the loss of a job, the breakdown of a significant relationship, the loss of one's home, or a bereavement. In the giving of good pastoral care it is essential to look for all potentially contributing factors.

All these factors may well play a part in the aetiology of an addictive episode or lifestyle, but pastors should be more concerned with the individual. There are many possible reasons for someone's addicted behaviour, and we may only discover these as we get to know the person better in our pastoral engagement with him or her and others who are involved, such as the immediate family.

The world of drugs and alcohol

In Erica James' novel *The Holiday*, addiction to drugs and alcohol plays a central role in the character of Mark. This is how she describes his descent into dependency on these two deceptive 'friends':

By his mid-twenties he had been drinking with a determined vengeance that had nothing to do with social drinking. It was warfare. A war against himself. It wasn't the taste he craved, it was the obliterating effect he needed: the desire to drink was as strong as the desire to eat, if not stronger. Seeking refuge in sleep – and a sleep in which he wasn't jerked awake by nightmares – he would fill himself with beer and whisky chasers until he collapsed on the bed and slept comatose for at least half the night.

Drugs came later, when desperation kicked in.

He had thought Kim was having an affair, but instead of confronting her, he put more energy into his drinking, until eventually, knowing he couldn't go on as he was, he turned to cocaine: It would slow him down and take the pressure off, he thought. But it didn't. In no time at all, he was addicted, not so much to the drug, but to the person he became when he was high. Without that buzz, he was nothing. A nobody. He got to the point where he couldn't get out of bed, or go to the local shop for a loaf of bread, unless his confidence had been fuelled by a line or two. What little sense of value he had soon went, as did his money.

Many people use alcohol on social occasions – an evening at the pub with friends, for example, or a couple of glasses of wine with a meal. This is not, generally speaking, symptomatic of a dangerous addiction. And most of us use drugs, regularly or occasionally. For someone with Type 1 diabetes, a regular supply of insulin is vital to health. A headache can usually be brought under control quite quickly with paracetamol. Even the caffeine in our breakfast coffee and tea is a drug.

We would not be worried about people taking necessary maintenance doses of insulin, or an occasional analgesic to deal with a relatively brief interlude of pain (equally, we might be wise to recognize such pain as a possible physiological response to overwork or excessive stress). Many of us use other substances such as vitamin supplements, which are freely available in pharmacies and even in newsagents. All these substances can be obtained either by prescription or 'over the counter'. But even with prescription drugs there is the possibility of addiction, particularly with regard to generic opioids and drugs like fentanyl, both of which are currently used in the symptom relief of some cancers and heart attack. These drugs are psychoactive, so their effect is psychological as well as physiological; this is what causes them, for some people, to become addictive, particularly because of the tolerance factor.

Alcohol can be easily obtained in most countries, at least if you are over 18 years old in the UK, and 21 in the USA. If I walk to my corner shop or visit a supermarket I can buy enough alcohol to damage my health very seriously indeed. To do this would be unwise, with its consequences for myself, my partner and my children and my work, and it would increase the likelihood of domestic or traffic-related accidents very considerably; it would, however, be perfectly legal to do so.

So-called 'recreational' drugs cannot be purchased as easily, and certainly not legally, in many countries including the UK; yet some people have argued that certain substances such as cannabis – used moderately – are less damaging than alcohol or cigarettes. That is one reason why countries such as the Netherlands and Portugal, and some states in the USA (most recently California) have changed their position on drugs such as cannabis in recent years. These substances can now be obtained and used legally in these places. Another reason has perhaps to do with the view that the 'war on drugs' has been a failure, and may even have done more harm than good by artificially increasing the price of such commodities, making it ever more profitable to produce and sell them, and causing those who buy them to fund addiction by crime. Despite the fact that the use of many types of non-prescription drugs is illegal, some UK cities now provide safe rooms where heroin users can inject or smoke drugs, in order to avoid public nuisance and danger from abandoned needles, and the spread of HIV and hepatitis through shared or carelessly discarded equipment. The arguments about all of these things continue, not least among healthcare professionals.

One aspect of drug misuse that has been very much in the news in recent years is the increase in addiction to prescription medication: that is to say, increasing dependence on a variety of drugs *that are obtained legally* via authorized medical practitioners. Rod Colvin's book *Prescription Drug Addiction, the Hidden Epidemic*, first published in 2002, describes this in detail, and was written partly in response to the death of his younger brother, from an overdose of prescription drugs and alcohol.

Part of the problem is the phenomenon of 'doctor-shopping', which happens in some countries, in which people who are hooked on these substances obtain them by going to a variety of doctors' surgeries and reporting a range of symptoms for which they request medication, but without any cross-checking between doctors to identify their habits.

So what kind of medication is misused in this way?

Colvin identifies three main categories of drugs that are involved in this fast-growing epidemic:

1 **Opioids,** such as Vicodin, Morphine and Methadone. These are used in legitimate medical practice to provide symptom control, particularly pain control. But they are also psycho-active, and have the potential to become addictive, through the processes of tolerance and withdrawal.
2 **Stimulants,** such as Adderall and Ritalin, which have the effect of calming in children, so they are sometimes used in cases of attention deficit disorder: but in adults they can have the opposite effect. That is to say, they stimulate the central nervous system.
3 **Sedatives,** such as Ativan, Valium, and a range of sleep inducing drugs. They have the opposite effect to the stimulants, by depressing the central nervous system. Used in legitimate medicine they help with anxiety and panic disorders, and with insomnia, but they too can be addictive.

There are two factors that make this type of addiction very difficult to work with. One is that – as with many addictions – there is the denial factor. Because people who are misusing prescription drugs are so dependent on them that they often find it very difficult to accept that they need help, this can be very problematic for the medical profession and their families and friends.

Second, many people who misuse drugs of this kind also drink excessive amounts of alcohol which makes their situation even more dangerous from a health perspective.

As with many conditions involving addiction to substances (and other kinds of addiction) it is of the greatest importance to find ways of enabling the person who has the addiction to recognize and accept that they are substance dependent and to find the help that is available. But this process is far from easy and may take a long time.

As Damian Thompson points out in his book *The Fix*, with the arrival of so many so-called 'legal highs' on the market world-wide, it is hard to maintain a distinction between drugs that are legally, or illegally, obtainable, and the same argument is increasingly applicable to the distinction between prescription and non-prescription drugs. This misuse of prescription drugs has reached a level that can properly be described as an epidemic.

So there is a lot of confusion about the role of alcohol and drugs in our world. They can be good for us, or at least neutral in their effect on our health, without going into questions relating to morality. In certain circumstances, they are clearly harmful.

Psychological therapists who work with addicted patients – particularly from a cognitive behavioural therapy (CBT) perspective – believe that identifying the causes of addiction for each individual can greatly enhance the prospects of cure. This relatively recent form of therapy aims to help people find ways of solving their own problems and so take better care of their own mental health. In the words of Stephen Briers in his book *Brilliant Cognitive Behavioural Therapy*, 'The essence of CBT is learning to challenge preconceptions about ourselves, other people and the world at large.' For it to be effective, there is a basic need to confront 'taken for granted or cherished convictions ... and examine them in the light of hard evidence'.[4] So the foundation of this clinical approach is *verifiability*. It has been used extensively in the UK for people experiencing a variety of psychological difficulties such as depression and anxiety. In the care of people with addictions, this therapeutic work is sometimes combined with the use of drugs like Librium™ to help clients cope with the anxieties that can arise when attempting to give up using a drug.

In reality, there may be as many reasons for addiction as there are addicted people, and the treatment given will always need to be tailored to the needs of the individual concerned.

The gate of heaven ...

For Christian ministers, all these potentially addictive substances have important spiritual implications, because they raise questions about what is good for the human body and what is truly harmful. If I enjoy a drink or smoking a joint, and there is no clear evidence that either of these taken in moderation is particularly harmful, then why not? And even if there is some risk, it could be argued that many ordinary human activities – some sports, for example – carry a degree of physical risk, but are in no sense generally seen as health threatening, anti-social or immoral. There are those, however, for whom the use of certain substances constitutes a serious health risk.

This book is concerned with *two* classes of such substances, *alcohol* and so-called *'illicit' drugs*, that is to say, drugs not usually available legally even on prescription – although there are many other forms of addiction, such as gambling, food or even sex. These two addictions are the ones pastors generally encounter in providing spiritual and pastoral care to their parishioners, whether they are members of their congregations or those who come to clergy houses to look for help – 'Knocking at Heaven's Door' as a report published by the Diocese of London describes it.

---

4 Stephen Briers, *Brilliant Cognitive Behavioural Therapy*, p. 10.

Alcohol and drug addiction, with their opportunities for pastoral care, are by no means confined to the inner-city areas with their visible contemporary 'binge-drinking' culture. Addiction is equally likely to be encountered in relatively prosperous suburban areas and in rural areas, although here the problems may well be more hidden, more containable, or more easily denied. 'They are not going to come to the vicar with these problems,' a suburban rector told me. 'They are much more likely to tell their GP – if anyone.'

Addiction – an illness?

Before going further and deeper into the causes of addiction and ways of treating addicted people clinically and pastorally, there is one important debate that I need to touch on briefly as it introduces a school of thought about addiction that we may find counterintuitive. Although we may regard this strange to consider or take seriously, there are those in the field of health-care psychology who deny that addiction exists at all; or if it does it should be regarded as a treatable disease. However, in his recent book *The Fix*, in which he writes about his own alcoholism and recovery, the journalist Damian Thompson casts considerable doubt on addiction treatments that are based on a disease model of substance dependency. And writing about so-called alcohol dependency, Herbert Fingarette argues:

> When behaviour is labelled a disease it becomes excusable because it is regarded as involuntary ... Thus special benefits are provided to alcoholics in employment, health and civil rights law provided they can prove that their drinking is persistent and heavy. The effect is to reward people who continue to drink heavily. This policy is insidious precisely because it is well intended, and those who criticise it may seem to lack compassion.[5]

---

5 Herbert Fingarette, in *Controversies in the Addiction's Field*, p. 52.

He concludes that it is better to see alcoholism (and by extension the same argument could, in principle, be applied to other
substance misuse) not as illness or disease, but as a problem
within our society. The use of alcohol, he says, has become one
way in which people who are facing difficult or acutely stressful
situations in our communities try to deal with their anxieties. If
this is so, attention to the underlying social and psychological
dynamics is far more likely to succeed than a programme of
labelling people who misuse alcohol as 'sick'. Such labelling is
for him a misleading and unscientific use of the word 'disease'.
While I totally agree with him that we are right to look at
the likelihood that alcohol misuse can be a strategy for coping
with life problems, I want to insist that addiction is in fact a
disease, and often needs clinical treatment.

The psychologist Jim Orford, who is similarly critical of
people who are sceptical of the 'disease model', argues that
people who deny the idea that addicts have an illness or disease do not adequately define the concept of disease. They
assume that addiction can only mean that an individual has
totally lost any control over his use of a substance, whereas it
is more realistic to define addiction as a *partial* loss of control.
Orford also helpfully argues for engagement with spiritual and
moral values as a pathway towards recovery.[6] He understands
addiction in terms of what he calls 'excessive appetite' which
can refer to a wide range of human behaviours, including the
misuse of drugs and alcohol. I find this expression very helpful
in thinking about how we can best define addiction.

On that basis, what is the best starting point for understanding and treating the truly addicted person?

It is helpful first to take a brief look at the neurological
system that is involved in the ingestion of drugs. The human
psyche is greatly influenced by *rewards and punishments*. At a

---

6 Jim Orford, *Excessive Appetites*. He talks about spiritual and
ethical approaches to addiction treatment in chapter 14. A good comprehensive discussion of 'disease' and 'choice' models of addiction can
be found in Robert West, *Theory of Addiction*.

psychological level we experience these things as *feelings*. At a neurological level the reward and punishment system is maintained in the brain by the neurotransmitters. Of these 'chemical messengers' within the brain's transport system, the hardest working are glutamates and GABA (gamma amino butyric acid). These function rather like green (glutamate) and red (GABA) lights in the brain – they either start or stop a process. For example, caffeine inhibits GABA release, thus operating like a green light and having an *arousing* effect on the brain; alcohol decreases glutamate activity and enhances GABA, so has a red light effect, causing a 'slow down' in the brain which we can experience as *relaxing*, at least on a temporary basis. Alcohol and drugs both have an effect on these processes, but it is thought that constant exposure to them in large quantities causes changes in the chemistry of the brain so that, in Gerald May's words, the nerve cells 'become less sensitive and responsive to repeated stimuli'.[7] One way of explaining this process is that the brain adapts to the taking of drugs, and so the unpleasant feelings of withdrawal are experienced when for one reason or another the drug of choice is unavailable.

All drugs (except benzodiazepines) that are misused by humans increase dopamine levels in the nucleus accumbens area of the brain. This part of the neurological system is thought to be involved in reward and motivation – and substance dependency. Taking sufficient quantities of a substance – such as coffee, alcohol or cannabis – operates as a *short cut* to obtaining a reward or eliminating an unpleasant or unwelcome feeling. Anyone who has used coffee to 'keep them going' or alcohol to help them relax will instantly recognize this process at an experiential level. We are taking a short cut to achieve a temporary reward that we would otherwise have to achieve in more time-consuming or demanding ways. But for some people the drug itself can have such a powerful effect on the brain that over time a process of physiological dependency can be set up. This, together with other factors such

---

7 Gerald May, *Addiction and Grace*, p. 75.

as psychological pressures, can put the drug in control of the person. Even so, it is hard to be precise about how this process really works, although we can all recognize its damaging impact on individuals and families.

So there can come a point for some people when dependence on this artificially stimulated reward system gets out of control, and that is when, arguably, addiction can start to replace a 'normal' enjoyment of the substance or activity in question – alcohol, cannabis, nicotine, gambling, sex, or even coffee or tea.

So – are addicts sick?

There are many ways of answering this question. They range from the belief on the one hand that addicted people are weak-willed, or sinful (to put it in religious terms), to the alternative view that the phenomenon of addiction has its origins in human biology. Genetic factors do cause a vulnerability that may predispose *some people* to addictive patterns of behaviour, but that is not, of course, to suggest that anyone who has this particular genetic pattern will *necessarily* become an addict. But those who are vulnerable through genetic factors may, if the circumstances of life become too difficult or stressful, or even boring, find that their use of drugs in order to provide relief or excitement can become increasingly uncontrollable.

From a pragmatic point of view, a number of agencies in our local communities offer treatment to people whose life has been damaged by dependence on excessive quantities of alcohol or the use of unauthorized mind-altering drugs. The use of the word 'treatment' means that these agencies usually work from the point of view that addiction is a treatable, though not necessarily curable, illness.

These national and local agencies – Alcoholics Anonymous, Narcotics Anonymous, and hospitals and clinics that treat addicted people – tend to take the view that people with addiction problems are basically *suffering*, and therefore need *treatment*. Once treatment has been given and the receiver of that treatment has started the process of recovery, the *hope* is that they then can begin to take control of their lives again and live in a way that brings them, and their families, greater fulfilment and happiness. It is, however, important to be realistic about what can be achieved and to be aware that there are high relapse rates, in some cases 70 to 80 per cent within the first year after treatment; many people with addictive lifestyles need to go into treatment far more than once, and for some sobriety will be a lifelong struggle. Equally, sometimes a *reduction* in substance misuse will be a far more realistic goal than *total abstinence*: some people will never be able to live a life of complete abstinence from alcohol or drugs.

These facts, in one way depressing and alarming, are important to pastors because they can help to relieve the burden of feeling that we 'ought to be able to help', or that we are in any way guilty of failing, if people who have had periods of sobriety regress and go back into the misuse of drugs or alcohol – as they very often do. Agencies such as the Maudsley Hospital that try to give medical help find exactly the same things happening, and often have to be content with making a limited or temporary difference to people's lives. This should be reassuring for all of us in our own attempts to help people out of substance dependence.

The concept of *control of one's own life* is fundamental in trying to understand the difference between the 'use' and 'misuse' of drugs and alcohol. *Who is in charge?* If it is the substance, then there is the likelihood of dependency. Once the individual has recognized and accepted that he is addicted, that is the time when treatment *may* be successfully given. However, many deny their substance dependency for years.

Is it addiction?

The majority of those who drink use alcohol in moderation, and by no means is every user of a 'recreational' drug an addict. The test for addiction relates principally to two factors that come into play when people are misusing these substances – the *withdrawal* factor and the *tolerance* factor.

Withdrawal, in a technical sense, refers to the acutely unpleasant symptoms that are associated with stopping drinking alcohol excessively or misusing drugs. In the case of an alcohol-dependent drinker, there may soon come a point where symptoms include physical shaking, nausea, dehydration and 'dry heaves' – attempted vomiting with little or no result. At a more advanced stage there can be severe neurological disorders including fits, and there can be a risk of death. This is a much more serious state of pathology than the experience of a hangover – and the temptation to go back to taking the substance that caused it. This will provide relief on a temporary basis. Most of us recognize and operate in the knowledge that this process is dangerous: however, the truly addicted user either cannot make that connection or has gone past the point where such considerations can influence his or her behaviour.

Tolerance occurs as people use drugs or alcohol (or other activities such as eating), either to achieve a certain enjoyable sensation or to relieve mental distress, and find that the amount needed to achieve these effects tends to increase. The substance user gradually comes to need more and more of the substance to achieve the same effect.

Here too there may be a threshold period during which it is possible for the substance user to recognize the danger signals. But when that has been passed, the likelihood is that he will move from being in control of his use of the substance to being controlled by it, and this is the point when addiction patterns often occur. So people who specialize in understanding and treating addiction have come to the view that tolerance and withdrawal factors lead addicted people into various forms of behavioural activities in order to deal with the situation. These activities relate to the time, effort and money spent in acquiring the 'goods', or the measures taken to relieve the withdrawal effects – such as taking more of the substance to reduce the pain arising from last night's drug or alcohol activity.

One important and obvious fact is that the use of alcohol and illicit drugs often originates in human desire for pleasurable experiences. People enjoy alcohol because they like the taste of beer or wine, the pleasant effect that it can produce when used in moderation, and the contribution it makes to social occasions, a fact recognized many centuries ago by writers such as Plato. It also plays a part in religious ceremonies such as the Jewish Passover meal and the Christian celebration of the Lord's Supper. So the use of alcohol for pleasure raises some issues about the nature of pleasure and desire within the history of Christian thought. Chapter 3 looks at the way in which the Christian Church understands the *virtuous* expression of desire and the pleasures of life as understood by some outstanding Christian writers, including Paul.

However, there is no doubt that misuse of some drugs, including alcohol, can have a destructive effect on people's physical, emotional and spiritual health, their family relationships, their work, and indeed every aspect of life. Drugs are evolving all the time, making them hard to police, and they can lead to serious health issues. Another point to note is that there is considerable disparity between countries in the views held about the beneficial and damaging effects of such substances.

2

Religion and Addiction: Religious Writing about Addiction from Gerald May Onwards

The American psychiatrist and writer on Christian spirituality Gerald May was the first person to tackle the subject of religion and addiction in a systematic way. His book *Addiction and Grace* (1988) was later followed by James Nelson's *Thirst: God and the Alcoholic Experience* (2004) and Christopher Cook's *Alcohol, Addiction and Christian Ethics* (2006). All three books have very important things to say about addiction and how we can help addicted people from a pastoral perspective. May was a pioneer in the field, and his insights are still full of wise guidance about the mysterious nature of addiction. Nelson speaks about his personal experience of being alcohol dependent and how he overcame it. Cook, taking an ethical line, makes a link between *personal* morality in relation to alcohol (and this has implications for other forms of substance dependency) and morality in the *public* arena: he concerns himself with questions about how societies can help to reduce the excessive consumption of addictive substances.

Gerald May, *Addiction and Grace*

In *Addiction and Grace*, Gerald May describes his experience of treating patients with dependency problems, such as the misuse of LSD, marijuana and cocaine. He also concerns himself with less obviously addictive substances such as generic analgesics, antidepressants and tranquillizers. But he also began to recognize dependency symptoms *in himself*, including attachment to 'nicotine, caffeine, sugar and chocolate, to name a few'. He also recognized his attachments to 'work, performance, responsibility, intimacy, being liked, helping others, and an almost endless list of other behaviors'. This is not to suggest that these things are essentially inappropriate goals in life, but he wants us to recognize that they can become attachments that, for the Christian in particular, can take the place of what is of ultimate significance, namely God. May regards the word 'addict' as an appropriate description of people who have such attachments, whether religious or not, and without being at all judgemental of them or of their lifestyle.

May lists the substances and activities that he regards as potentially addictive,[1] including alcohol and drugs, and he divides these activities into two classes, which he defines as *attraction* addictions and *aversion* addictions. Attraction addictions are those where a substance or activity such as gambling has a high positive value for the individual; aversion addictions are those in which the individual puts compulsive effort into avoidance – of anger, for example. May points out that although many of these activities may seem to be positive (such as a mother's love for her children), a line can be crossed at which point the activity specified has become an addiction rather than something freely chosen. As May puts it, '*no* addiction is good; *no* attachment is beneficial'.[2] This is because addictions are aspects of functioning that limit human freedom, and they act, in the specifically spiritual sense, as barriers between the person and God.

So how does addiction happen? May pays particular attention to the idea of *attachment*: 'It comes from the old French *attaché*, meaning "nailed to". Attachment "nails" our desire to specific objects and creates addiction.'[3] This is the core of his argument. These attachments 'enslave us with chains that are

---

1 Gerald May, *Addiction and Grace*, pp. 38–9.
2 May, *Addiction*, p. 39.
3 May, *Addiction*, p. 3.

of our own making and yet that, paradoxically, are virtually beyond our control'.

May describes addiction as a psychological process in which there is a splitting of the will into two, so that part of it wants to continue the activity and another part wants to give it up: a conflict is then set up that in turn damages self-esteem. Paradoxically, this undermining process is strengthened by the attempts people make to relinquish addictive behaviour but fail to do so. So addiction arises partly out of the attempt to control certain forms of behaviour such as the use of drugs or alcohol, and partly from the awareness of the individual of his inability to do so. This process is central to May's attachment argument, and the psychological aspect of addiction is reinforced by chemical dependencies that involve changes in the neurological structures of the brain through long-term substance use.

Analysing this process further, May identifies a number of what he describes as 'mind tricks' that promote or reinforce addictive forms of behaviour. For him these take two principal forms: *self-deception*, such as denial, and *collusion*, when others avoid confronting the addicted person and so do not try to help him find a way out of his slavery.

Although he does not define the moment at which a person's use of a substance has become compulsive, May makes the important point that we all stand at risk of becoming over-attached. This is highly significant, as it rejects the mistaken idea that there are addicts and there are people who do not have what are sometimes erroneously called 'addictive personalities' – there really is no 'them' and 'us'. Any of us, particularly when faced with situations that threaten or deeply disturb us, could become attached to substances or activities in a way that could be described as addictive.

After describing the psychological mechanisms and neurological aspects of attachment, *Addiction and Grace* provides a method of helping those whose lives have been damaged by addiction to find freedom from their predicament. This method, unlike those offered by specifically medical models of care, concentrates on looking for a *spiritual* approach to healing and liberation, one that is based on the availability of *divine grace*.

May takes as his starting point not the situation that occurs when human beings 'lose their way' – as, for example, in severe cases of addiction to drugs – but the *ideal situation*, the Garden of Eden described in Genesis before human rebellion against God had converted it into what May calls 'an empty and idolatrous wasteland'.[4] This is how May expounds his theory of grace in relation to addiction. This quotation clearly expresses what he is trying to demonstrate:

> Grace is the active expression of God's love. God's love is the root of grace; grace itself is the dynamic flowering of this love; and the good things that result in life are the fruit of this divine process. Grace appears in many ways, which theologians have attempted to categorize ... Jesus spoke of God as being our intimate, loving parent, and he wished for us to receive God's love like little children.[5]

The ideal relationship between God and humanity, described as having the characteristics of a parent–child interaction, recognizes that human approaches to God are often contaminated by attempts to manipulate God, just as children try to manipulate their human parents. By way of contrast, however, God does not control human beings: 'God calls us, invites us, and even commands us, but God does not control our response. We bear responsibility for the choices we make.'[6] This sentence has a great deal of significance in our attempt to understand addiction. Although in the early stages of substance dependency the individual can make choices, and so be held responsible for the decision to start or stop the activity concerned, there comes a stage in the process of becoming substance dependent when

---

4 May, *Addiction*, p. 119.
5 May, *Addiction*, p. 120.
6 May, *Addiction*, p. 122.

free choice has been largely eroded by the substance and its constitutional effects on the psyche.

May looks at the ways in which the potential for a grace-filled relationship between God and humanity can be compromised. At such times, May suggests, the 'immanent God in us becomes wounded with us, suffers, struggles, hopes, and creates with us'.[7] The locus of this reciprocal process is to be found in the Christian church community, where grace is something that is not predominantly or exclusively a private matter, but finds its expression in the life of that community.[8] This is a most important contribution to the understanding of the worshipping community as a place where channels of healing for addicted people could be available wherever there is in church communities an open and non-judgemental attitude to people with drug-related or other addictions. This is an aspect of May's thought that I find particularly important and helpful as it invites church members to take addictions seriously, despite the difficulties and challenges of what can seem like a very dark and difficult aspect of human life – cunning, powerful and baffling, as AA expresses it. Although May does not look at this in detail it is something I want to encourage, and that is one reason for writing this book. Chapter 4 is devoted to a discussion of the pastoral care of people who are addicted.

With regard to grace, May tells us that grace can never be earned; it can only be received as a divine gift. Human beings cannot succeed in manipulating the 'God-parent'. Grace and its reception cannot therefore be controlled. Here again, there is a link with addiction theory, because addicted people often attempt to control or manipulate their environment through alcohol, drugs, or other forms of addicted behaviour, to produce immediate effects of pleasure or the relief of pain.

---

7 May, *Addiction*, p. 124.

8 Although May is speaking here from a Christian point of view, and using Christian Scripture to illustrate his ideas, it is important to recognize that the same could be said of other, non-Christian, faith communities.

In asserting God's freedom in the gift of grace, May is not, however, suggesting that human beings can only be passive in their receptivity. There is space for an active approach, in which prayer plays a part by 'requesting' grace from God, in a way that prepares the soul to receive and act upon grace. According to May, grace has a part to play in the healing process for people who are suffering from addictions.

The person who is, to use a well-known expression in the world of addiction healthcare, at 'rock bottom', has only two possible choices. One is to stay in that helpless position, the other is to turn towards anything that can hold out the hope of change, however small and unpromising that hope may seem to be. This is what May means by the word *faith*. In using this word he is not referring to giving personal assent to a set of creedal propositions or statements about God so much as to engagement with *risk*. The content of that risk, in terms of faith, is the possibility of *trust*.

But this kind of trust is not what might be called a leap in the dark, because *it involves returning to patterns of trusting behaviour that have proved helpful in the past*, and which therefore offer similar reliability in the present. This experience of trust can be, so to speak, programmed into the brain, and so the 'cells of the brain become more accepting of it'.[9] So we can predict that behaviour which has provided assistance in the past will be found helpful again, and this trust has to do with relationships: a belief that God will not let down or abandon human beings no matter how low and despondent they may have become, and that fellow human beings will also meet the needs of the person with the addiction. This is a dynamic process, he suggests: 'For each layer of trust that builds up, another, more challenging risk is offered.'[10]

A reciprocal relationship then, lies at the heart of faith and trust: on the one hand there is the offering that God continually makes, and on the other the human response, a movement

9 May, *Addiction*, p. 124.
10 May, *Addiction*, p. 130.

of the heart at least as much as of the mind, but which must be given freely and without constraint.

For May it is when we are at our most helpless and vulnerable, in what he refers to as a spiritual 'desert', that we are most open to the reception of grace. 'The desert', he writes, 'is where the battle with attachment takes place. The saga of the desert tells of a journey out of slavery, through the desert, toward the garden that is home.'[11] This journey involves 'purgation and purification' and a 'loving courtship, a homemaking between the human soul and its Creator'. This experience, he suggests, is one that all people have, but it is brought into a particularly sharp focus through the experience of addictive behaviour. In all cases the same struggle is involved, and the journey, if completed well enough, leads from the slavery of the desert of attachment to the freedom of that 'garden that is home'.

May is, however, under no illusions about the hardship and the cost of that journey:

> At its mildest, the desert is a laboratory where one learns something about addiction and grace. In more fullness, it is a testing ground where faith and love are tried by fire. And with grace, the desert can become a furnace of real repentance and purification where pride, complacency, and even some of the power of attachment can be burned away, and where the rain of God's love can bring conversion: life to the seeds of freedom.[12]

This sense of a hard journey, and a purging of desire through a furnace, is illustrated with reference to the lives of well-known spiritual leaders, including 'Elijah and other great Hebrew prophets', the saints of Hinduism, Buddhism, especially in the person of Gautama, John the Baptist, the Christian desert mothers and fathers, Muhammad, and of course Jesus, particularly in his own temptation story in a deserted, wilderness environment. Most of these historic figures did not *choose*

---

11 May, *Addiction*, p. 133f.
12 May, *Addiction*, p. 137.

their 'desert' experiences; conversely, they were chosen, and in positive response to their calling were obliged to test their vocation in the desert.

In the case of Jesus, May suggests, we have a most important illustration of the relationship between attachment and the possibility of overcoming it, in the specific context of the temptation accounts in the Synoptic Gospels.[13] Each episode in the account speaks of the problem of attachment: in Satan's invitation to turn stone into bread there is a temptation to 'play god' – to misuse power for personal gain; in the temptation to jump off the Temple parapet the issue is one of manipulation; the invitation to become master of the world is the temptation to put personal power in the place of God – in theological language, the ultimate act of idolatry.[14]

The nature of that idolatry is that in the temptations, 'Satan was hoping Jesus would fall prey to attachment: attachment to meeting his own needs, attachment to his own power, or attachment to the material riches of the world'.[15] In his full humanity, Jesus was undergoing a real ordeal, not an imaginary one, and all human beings who are tempted to fall into attachment behaviour patterns have to undergo that same ordeal, meeting it with the same resources available to Jesus, primarily those of humility and trusting faith. In that act of faith, there comes the reality of *empowerment*.

It is a long time since Gerald May wrote his helpful and imaginative book, with its important insights into what was then a poorly understood aspect of human distress. He addresses the questions with the wisdom and experience of a practising psychiatrist and a religious writer, although he helpfully reminds us that he is not a professional theologian. He is honest enough to recognize that he also had to face addictive tendencies in himself, in his need to overwork and the compulsive desire to

---

13 In fact, the word 'testing' is probably nearer in meaning than 'temptation' to the Greek verb *peirazo* which is used by all three evangelists (Mark 1.12–13; Matthew 4.1–11; Luke 4.1–13).

14 May, *Addiction*, p. 138.

15 May, *Addiction*, p. 138.

be valued or admired. He did not include any reflections on the possibility of genetic factors in his book: that part of the picture did not emerge till much later.

There is something unsatisfactory about May's tendency to identify addiction with human attachments, in the sense that if we are all attached to something, then on his terms we might all be regarded as addicts. But his suggestion that the grace he speaks of is not only an aspect of the relationship between an individual and God but also something that can be effective in a person's life through membership of a church, with its worship, sacraments and non-judgemental pastoral care, comes as a welcome insight. There is in this thought great potential for pastoral and spiritual ministry.

Perhaps one of May's most important insights is that all addiction has a social context. There can be a lot of pressure in our society, particularly perhaps on young people, to make use of alcohol and drugs; these things are for the most part available, affordable and socially acceptable. Many can resist these temptations but some find that particularly hard, perhaps most of all at times of personal change or vulnerability. We are wise to see that addiction often comes about when people are exposed to situations in which they are under a great deal of stress, such as the loss of a job or a home, or the ending of a significant relationship through separation or death. For pastors, it is often through understanding these life events and crises and helping the person through them that they can also help the individual to avoid or if necessary overcome the misuse of alcohol or drugs.

James B. Nelson, *Thirst, God and the Alcoholic Experience*

James Nelson, a minister of the United Church of Christ in the USA, became well known in theological circles in the late 1970s when he began to write on the subject of Christianity and 'embodiment', particularly in terms of human sexuality.

Thirst, his work on alcoholism published in 2004, has the considerable advantage of being written by someone whose own life was almost ruined by alcohol. So it has the passion and commitment of an author who knows his subject not just from academic study but from self-observation and his own personal way out of that particular form of 'slavery'.

Nelson explores the disease concept of addiction, recognizing that if addiction (to alcohol, for example) is a *disease*, then the person affected by it cannot be blamed for having it: and treatment for it needs to take that into account. If on the other hand addiction is a *choice*, then it may be legitimately seen, from a religious perspective, as a sinful form of behaviour. Nelson's analysis is particularly helpful in that he writes not as an outsider to the world of the addict, but as a 'recovering alcoholic', with developing insight into his own condition. While there is perhaps a danger of generalizing on the basis of this autobiographical information, his frankness and self-disclosure puts his work into a very different category from that of the spectator, however sympathetic.

This is how Nelson describes the process of his own addiction:

> Both stimulation and blessed calm came from the coffee cup and the pipe. But alcohol? I had not the slightest inkling that I would become addicted and certainly did not intend that. No one ever does. The cost of membership in that club is just too high.
>
> When I began to use alcohol moderately and regularly, I did so because (for a variety of reasons) it made me feel good. After some years, however, I depended on alcohol not just to feel good but to feel *normal*. Finally there came the 'oops phenomenon' – the surprising, wrenching realization that I was hooked.[16]

---

16 James Nelson, *Thirst*, p. 37. The term 'oops phenomenon' is attributed by Nelson to an article by Alan Leshner, 'Addiction: A Brain Disease with Biological Underpinnings', *The Voice*, Winter 2001.

This highlights a number of very important insights into addiction. The least contentious statement in this analysis of his own experience is the assertion that he 'certainly did not intend' to become an alcoholic, because 'no one ever does'. He points out that the process of becoming a dependent drinker rather than a controlled drinker is 'deceptively gradual', so that 'even those close to us can seldom help us. The change becomes hurtful before they realize it, and they withdraw from us in confusion, pity, or disgust.'[17]

Nelson's understanding of the causes of alcoholism

Nelson takes seriously the influence of hereditary factors as one of the causes of alcohol dependence:

> I find the cumulative evidence persuasive. Regarding alcoholism, while genes do not *predetermine* anything, it strongly appears that they do *predispose*. Though my own parents were abstinent, there was alcoholism elsewhere on both sides of the family.[18]

So although he recognizes the contribution that heritability makes to alcoholism, genetic influence alone will not be sufficient to cause alcohol or other substance dependency: there have to be other complementary factors. These he describes as 'psychological and emotional, sociological and cultural, the religious and the spiritual'.[19]

Looking at the psychological dimension to this, Nelson speaks of his own experience of using alcohol in order to provide pain relief. He describes his struggles with hyperactivity, highlighting the excessive self-criticism and low self-esteem that underlay his increasingly pathological relationship with alcohol. In his analysis of these feelings he noticed his sense

---

17 Nelson, *Thirst*, p. 38.
18 Nelson, *Thirst*, p. 39.
19 Nelson, *Thirst*, p. 39.

of being at risk of being unmasked as a 'fraud', and yet being unable to speak of these fears with anyone else. Alcohol was for him one way of anaesthetizing these painful emotions. He speaks of using psychotherapy to explore childhood issues that had helped to produce these conflicts, which seem to have been caused by his family's 'heavy-handed authoritarianism, success-worship, moralism and overt rejection'. This therapy was helpful, but it did not prevent him from using alcohol to provide additional relief from tension. The problem with this kind of relief drinking is, as Nelson rightly observes, that in time the drinking sets up a 'vicious self-feeding cycle of increased drinking to overcome the painful effects of previous excessive drinking'.[20]

There is, however, a welcome reluctance in Nelson's book to be too hasty in producing a comprehensive 'causatory' theory of addiction, and he persuasively argues that we will never get to the roots of substance dependency without allowing for the *mysterious and paradoxical* element in addiction. From personal encounters with recovering alcoholics I am aware that this element has an important role to play in the work of organizations such as Alcoholics Anonymous, and it is no accident that these organizations have more investment than other helpers often do in the use of spiritual and religious ideas in their understanding of the paradoxical problems of addiction and the route that needs to be taken towards recovery, in which spiritual support and guidance often play an important role.

On sociological and cultural factors, Nelson points to one of the most neglected factors in the origins of alcohol dependence, that of the social approval of the use of alcohol. Different societies (and religions) view alcohol use very differently. Europe generally views alcohol use with acceptance and tolerance, while countries where Islam is the main or only religion, such as Iran or Saudi Arabia, view its consumption with extreme official disapproval. Among the risk factors

---

20 Nelson, *Thirst*, p. 40.

he discusses, Nelson attaches importance to the fact that he is 'male, of Scandinavian descent, and a city dweller' – all described as risk factors. The availability, social approval and affordability of alcohol all play their part. On the other hand, many people who have been exposed in equal measure to these risk factors do not become alcoholic, so there must, Nelson argues, be other factors at work.

'Disease' and 'sin' explanations of alcoholism

Nelson suggests five possible ways of looking at the evidence for the view that alcoholism and other addictive behaviours are diseases rather than a chosen way of life, which some writers with a religious background might refer to as 'sinful'.

1 *It's purely sin.* This is the most extreme position from a religious perspective. The behaviour is freely chosen, for reasons of human sinfulness.
2 *It begins as sin and becomes disease.* This is a modified form of the previous one. He mentions two radically different religious bodies, the Salvation Army (drinking is wrong) and the Roman Catholic Church (excessive drinking is wrong) and suggests that these two churches share the view that what begins as a choice can become a compulsion.
3 *Addiction is sin and disease all mixed together.* This is the Alcoholics Anonymous position. There is a convergence between moral failure and chemical dependency.
4 *Addiction is disease resulting from sin, but that sin is outside a person's responsibility.* Sin is seen here as a matter not so much of personal choice as of the reality of living in sinful societies that are abusive and exploitative, whether in terms of family dysfunction, sexism, racism or poverty. In such societies where substance dependency is prevalent the ability of the disturbed individual to avoid addiction is eroded – he or she is to some extent a *victim*.
5 *Addiction is purely disease; sin is not a factor.* This is the opposite extreme to position 1. It takes the view that a per-

centage of those who drink are 'biologically programmed' to become addicted to alcohol, given a set of life experiences that influence the process of becoming addicted. Where there is no real choice, to talk of sin is meaningless.

Alcoholism as a disease

Nelson identifies five criteria for viewing alcoholism as a disease (and similar arguments could be used about other substances).

1 Alcoholism fits the criteria for a disease and has been defined as such by leading medical and health organizations.
2 Alcoholism as a disease is marked by brain changes that explain otherwise inexplicable behaviour.
3 The disease concept helps us to distinguish between cause and effect.
4 Understanding alcoholism as a disease markedly undercuts moralistic judgements and blaming, thus enhancing the chances for recovery.
5 The disease theory reduces our tendency to see evil as 'out there' and external to ourselves.

The first point, alcoholism viewed as a disease, is a matter of fact, in the sense that it has been classified as a disease by the World Health Organization and the American Medical Association. The second, relating to brain changes, depends on the notion of chemical change in the brain brought about by its exposure to alcohol in certain amounts. Nelson, along with many other addiction theorists, believes that chemical changes caused by long-term use of alcohol gradually reduce the ability of the alcoholic to give up using it.

On the third point, from the standpoint of cause and effect, the argument is between those who say that people drink because they are alcoholics and those who claim that people become alcoholics because they drink too much. This is complicated, because there are people who often exceed the prevailing recommended daily alcohol allowance without showing symptoms of true dependency – this raises the question of how dependency can be defined in contrast to 'normal' use of alcohol.[21] An amount that would tip the scales for one person might fail to do so for another: as Nelson points out, '*any* alcohol was too much for me'.

The fourth point refers to the advantages, from a treatment perspective, that come when the alcoholic is not seen as someone who has behaved immorally, irresponsibly or sinfully. There might well be a better chance for recovery for someone who is treated as a patient rather than as a sinner – although that might not necessarily be a universal truth. For someone who believes herself to be culpable, a healthy recognition of that could be beneficial: one treatment goal can often be to help the 'client' to be more truthful about herself and the relationships that have been adversely affected by substance or activity dependent behaviour. And we may wonder whether it is true, as Nelson suggests, that the non-judgemental approach actually enhances 'the chances for recovery'. There seems to be little hard evidence for this, and recovery is often a complex process with many beginnings and endings; on the other hand, it may be true that a non-judgemental approach helps some people to take the first step of seeking treatment, whether or not that treatment is ultimately successful. We may find ourselves wondering here to what extent Nelson's argument may be skewed because of his own experience.

The fifth point is less contentious in religious terms. The temptation to see only good within oneself and evil as somehow external to the self is clearly a fallacy in religious discourse, going back in the Hebrew literature to the theology of the scapegoat.[22] This finds a modern echo, as Nelson poignantly observes, in racist and sexist behaviour. In the case of alcoholic behaviour, it may sometimes be that some churches scapegoat

---

21 The same criteria would have traction in relation to other forms of substance ingestion (including coffee, for example) and potentially addictive activities such as shopping or gambling.

22 Nelson for this purpose cites Leviticus 16.21.

people in their congregations who are addicted rather than approaching them with empathy and understanding.

Against those healthcare psychologists who reject the whole concept of addiction, Nelson presents a counter-claim:

> Even though the scientific evidence for alcoholism as disease is still less complete than it currently is for some other illnesses, something significant has been happening: the disease concept itself has stimulated scientific research, which in turn has established the concept even more securely among medical professionals and the public.[23]

As with many other illnesses, the reality of the condition is there long before it can be named – giving it a name helps those who are investigating it to be clear about their task of trying to understand it and providing a cure where possible.

Nelson considers other objections to regarding alcoholism as a disease, such as the argument that this can have the negative effect of taking away the responsibility of the person with the problem for trying to overcome it. In the face of this objection, Nelson introduces the important matter of *denial*. Far from attributing their situation to genetic or circumstantial causes, alcoholics often deny to themselves and to others that they have a problem. Nelson's reflections on his own alcoholism lead him to say: 'I staunchly denied my alcoholism to the end. My increasingly heavy drinking was due to the dynamics of the disease itself, including organic brain changes. It was not due to a feeling of genetic fatalism.'[24]

Taking a 'Platonic' line, Nelson argues that there is 'Sin' as an idea, and individual 'sins' as instances of that reality. Beneath the things that alcoholics do that are sinful in nature, then, there is an underlying reality, which Nelson tries to identify. That reality is to be found in four behaviours: perfectionism, control, selfishness and attachment. He recalls that AA's founders saw selfishness as a given of the human

23 Nelson, *Thirst*, p. 52.
24 Nelson, *Thirst*, p. 56.

condition, something that all great religions have attempted to transcend but never have completely. Hence its destructiveness should be minimized, but its continuing reality should be honestly acknowledged as it is from this selfish basis that artificial attachments spring, whether to people, objects or behaviours.

At this point Nelson, with echoes of the thought world of Paul Tillich, whom he quotes at several points, describes sin as ultimately a form of *estrangement*, and this is of great importance. 'It is relational brokenness, separation from everything meaningful. It is alienation from ourselves, from those around us, and from our environment. Fundamentally it is estrangement from God, the source and ground of all that exists.'[25] Furthermore, although he rejects some of the more moralistic views of Augustine (on sexual matters, for example), and the idea of sin as biologically transmitted, he suggests that sin is transmitted from one person to another *in societies* through attitudes to the material world that encourage the wrong kind of dependence on created things. On this Nelson comments perceptively:

> Perceiving original sin as estrangement that is conveyed by social means was an important new perspective in the early twentieth century. It is no less relevant to a twenty-first century culture where instant gratification is taken almost as a right and where one corporate slogan, 'Better living through chemistry' has become emblematic for society as a whole.[26]

This leads Nelson to the idea that addiction can be viewed as a form of *idolatry*. Tillich describes as 'heteronomy' any idolatrous worldview that places anything other than God at the centre of its concerns. The spiritual and pastoral aspect of this then becomes the process of restoring God to God's proper place in the hierarchy of human values.

In the last chapter of his book, Nelson draws extensively on John's Gospel, where there is much emphasis on truth as a

---

25 Nelson, *Thirst*, p. 67.
26 Nelson, *Thirst*, p. 69.

liberating, life-giving, life-restoring force. Truth is more than something that 'is', it is actually something dynamic that we 'do'. That 'doing' process must then include the reversal of the *dynamic of denial* that I mentioned earlier. To recognize this truth is the beginning of a realization that drinking to excess (or any other addiction) is a form of slavery – and the capacity for awareness of this generates a 'thirst for the truth that would make me free'. Every pastor who has worked with addicted people (and their families) will know the reality of this, and the painful process by which the alcoholic reaches the moment of decision – often forced on him by circumstances of health or social disintegration – that leads to the acknowledgement of his need for help. Tragically, not every addict makes this acknowledgement, but when they do, grace is available; as Nelson recognizes, the centrality of the cross in Christian theology is the point at which, despite the horrors of many forms of abuse and misuse of God's gifts, there is 'a compelling revelation of the gracious Heart of the Universe'.[27]

There is little here that clarifies the distinction between normal and abnormal use of drugs or alcohol: maybe Nelson is so aware of the impossibility of his ever returning to controlled drinking that he doesn't really allow for this distinction. The book is on surest ground when the locus of addiction is seen not just, or even principally, as a matter of the individual, but as a sign of a society in which instant gratification is taken as a 'human right', and the damage that this philosophy can do when that supposed right involves the use of potentially addictive commodities such as alcohol.

In his book *Practical Theology*, Richard Osmer comments that although not everyone would accept the 'disease model' of addiction, Nelson's identification of the complexity of understandings of addiction – genetic, psychological and sociological – is to be welcomed. This supports the theory that there is no simple answer to why people become addicted. The task of providing helpful treatment, of whatever kind, is a complex

---

27 Nelson, *Thirst*, p. 165.

undertaking, one that frequently reveals itself in a tortuous and often baffling and paradoxical manner.

Is addiction incurable, particularly when it takes the form of alcohol dependency? This seems to be the view that Nelson takes of his own condition. Tony Adams, a former captain of the England football team who has written of his experiences of addiction holds a similar view. Like Nelson he describes himself as an alcoholic. Adams regards this description rather in the way that another person might describe himself as 'a diabetic'. Both Nelson and Adams believe that the alcohol-dependent drinker is 'an alcoholic for life' and will need to exercise perpetual vigilance lest this disease, 'cunning, powerful and baffling', should recur and cause further physiological, psychological and relational damage even many years after the individual has come to believe himself to be abstinent. Adams writes of looking for AA meetings to attend wherever he travelled to play football for his club or country.

Yet we may perhaps wonder whether this approach is necessarily one that is needed by all who have an episode of alcoholic dependency. Other types of treatment do not make assumptions about the 'alcoholic' or 'drug addict' *for life* diagnosis, regarding this process as labelling that may not help the individual towards personal empowerment and positive self-evaluation. This can be true even when people with dependency problems are referred many times to detoxification or rehabilitation units, and may never completely break the cycle of dependency. There is a controversy, then, about this 'for life' element, perhaps related to the potential disadvantage to an individual of regarding herself as having a disease that is lifelong, like diabetes. I mention this because of the ongoing debate about these issues that has not so far been resolved. It may well be that the most we can say confidently is that there is no 'one-size-fits-all' answer that will work with all addicted people; in both clinical and pastoral intervention we need to tailor our response to the needs of individuals.

Christopher Cook, *Alcohol, Addiction and Christian Ethics*

Christopher Cook is professorial research fellow in the Department of Theology and Religion at the University of Durham. He is a consultant psychiatrist who worked at the Institute of Psychiatry in south-east London, specializing originally in genetic factors in understanding addiction. He was ordained as an Anglican priest in 2001 in the Diocese of Canterbury. He therefore has understanding and experience on the subject of addiction from the perspective of the healthcare sciences, and combines that with his understanding of Christian theology and spirituality, which is particularly evident in his work on the *Philokalia*.[28]

His ethical outlook comes to the fore in *Alcohol, Addiction and Christian Ethics*, as his title makes clear. Of great importance for Cook is not just the question of individual responsibility for the use and misuse of alcohol, but also the question of public policy. In respect of the public aspects of addiction, for example, he concerns himself with the ambiguous relationship between the alcohol production and sales industry and the need for the government in the UK to derive sizeable revenue from taxation of the sales of alcohol, which arguably creates a conflict of interests.

Cook believes that it is of great importance to see addiction, from a theological perspective, as originating in an inner conflict that is part of the human condition. This phenomenon of conflict features in Paul's Epistle to the Romans, chapter 7, although there are many possible interpretations of this chapter, particularly verses 19–25, some of which are discussed by Cook in his chapter on 'Addiction as sin and syndrome'.

---

28 The *Philokalia* is an extensive collection of texts on the spiritual life emanating from the Orthodox Churches from the fourth to the fifteenth centuries. Cook's particular contribution to the study of these writings is concerned with the relationship between the *Philokalia* and mental health.

Clearly many people, from a variety of faith backgrounds or with no overt religious belief, drink far more alcohol than is consistent with their own health and social well-being and that of their families. However, substance-dependent people often have an awareness that excessive use of a substance is a problem on the one hand, but an inability to be more moderate on the other. Cook provides a detailed analysis of this paradox, and sees it in terms of Pauline and Augustinian theologies of the *divided self*, and the conflict between a wish to do what is in the best interests of the individual and society as a whole, and a desire to drink or use drugs excessively.

Cook considers the work of four theological writers in presenting a theological understanding of addiction: Paul, Augustine of Hippo, Thomas Aquinas and Martin Luther – all highly important Christian commentators on human behaviour and the theological and ethical issues surrounding the use of alcohol from different eras of the history of the Church.

Paul

In his letter to the Christian church in Rome, dated approximately 50 CE, Paul directs his attention to the phenomenon of what Cook refers to as the 'divided self':

> We know that the law is spiritual; but I am carnal, sold under sin. I do not understand my own actions. For I do not do what I want, but I do the very thing that I hate.[29]

Cook is careful to point out, however, that: 'The divided self of Romans 7:14–15 is ... not a description of addiction; it is a description of another kind of experience.'[30]

The section of the letter that contains chapter 7 builds up to a climactic expression of faith, to be revealed in the following

---

29 Romans 7.14–15, RSV.
30 Christopher Cook, *Alcohol, Addiction and Christian Ethics*, p. 143.

chapters. At this point, Paul is setting the scene for what he intends ultimately to say. He is addressing an audience that has come to faith in Christ from a variety of faith communities. Some church members are of Jewish origin, others are not. Paul respects the traditions that *all* have brought with them, and avoids any suggestion that one group has any ultimate advantage over another – and to this extent he is on a theological knife-edge. He refutes the suggestion that the Jews are deficient in their understanding of the range of God's promises by asserting the benefits that the Jews have because of their foundation on the Law and the Prophets, as we see, for example, in 3.1–4. This assertion is immediately balanced in 3.9 and 3.21ff., where it is made clear that just as all have in some sense failed in God's eyes, so his offer of forgiveness and grace through Jesus Christ as gifts available through faith is available to all – on equal terms.

Paul is therefore arguing for *religious inclusiveness* with a view to making it possible for the Roman Church of his day to include people of Jewish and non-Jewish religious traditions on an equal basis. This context is vital to a proper understanding of what the apostle is trying to achieve. He is to this extent a politician as well as a theological writer. But we are faced in Romans 7 with writing that appears to address some kind of inner debate that faces the individual believer, whatever their religious beliefs and practices before conversion. It is a passage that has in the past been thought to address human desires and how they may be *aligned with* the will of God as understood by the believer or *contrary to* that will. This understanding remains relevant in the work of some contemporary scholars. Cook addresses the interpretation of the Romans passage with reference to several significant commentators.

C. E. B. Cranfield is one of a number of New Testament scholars who see these verses as a reflection of what happens to the baptized Christian who finds himself growing spiritually through the work of the Holy Spirit; at the same time, however, sin will maintain some power over the individual, and this will never be fully resolved in this life because, as Cook puts it, 'even his best actions will always be marred by egotism'.[31]

Another biblical scholar, J. G. D. Dunn, is also convinced that the Romans passage about conflict refers to the post-conversion Christian, in whom a process of setting free the ego from sinful acts has started but is not yet complete. So the cry of Romans 7 is one of frustration between the pull of the world of the flesh and that of the new epoch of life in Christ, lived in the power of God. Dunn makes the point that there is for the Christian 'confidence in the deliverance that will come in Christ'.[32]

But Cook tells us that there is a competing school of thought, which says that these verses in Romans are about people who are not, or not yet, converted to Christianity. Those who take this view do not believe that in Paul's thought people living under the regime of Christ could be as sinful ('sold under sin') as the alternative explanation of Dunn and Cranfield suggests.

Cook presents his readers with a selection from a highly complex set of competing understandings about the Romans 7 passage. Interestingly he also introduces a different approach from the world of psychology, referring to the work on Paul done by Gerd Theissen in his book *Psychological Aspects of Pauline Theology*. Theissen uses the ancient Greek story of Medea, who kills her children to take revenge on her errant husband Jason, to illustrate the true meaning of the Romans passage, which for him reveals a tension either between desire and reason, or perhaps more realistically between two competing emotions, in this case love and anger. Theissen sees Paul's writing in Romans as drawing on the Medea tragedy, though he does not mention it specifically. What it leads to for Theissen is the idea of 'three tribunals' in which, as Cook quotes Theissen, 'the tribunal of the "I" stands between the antagonistic tribunals of the law which points to God, and the law of sin'.[33] This idea of competing desires in the mind is theo-logically based, but also draws on modern psychologies, which

31 Cook, *Alcohol*, p. 138.
32 Cook, *Alcohol*, p. 139.
33 Cook, *Alcohol*, p. 141.

from Freud onwards have based their personality theories on the importance of internal conflict.

It is not possible to go into greater detail here, but what emerges even from this brief survey is a sense that conflict between the will of God as understood by Christians and the will to disobey it is a strong force in human life. And as we are primarily concerned with addiction in this book, the Romans passage has an important contribution to make, because it tries to understand the phenomenon of competing desires: in the case of addiction to drugs and alcohol, this is the dilemma of two incompatible things – the desire to continue the use, or misuse, of these substances, and a comparable desire to give up their use.

Augustine of Hippo

The second writer chosen by Cook as a voice on the issue of self and conflicting desires is Augustine of Hippo. He discusses the use that Augustine makes, in Book VIII of the *Confessions* for example, of the idea of the divided will, in contrast perhaps to Paul's preference for the concept of the divided self:

> It becomes clear here that Augustine understood himself as possessing two wills in opposition to each other. The one will commanded that his mind should will that he follow the example of Victorinus. This was evident in his conscious-ness of 'commanding' himself to do the same. The other will was his unwillingness to follow Victorinus. This was evident in the fact that the 'command' was not actually obeyed. He understands this state of affairs as reflecting an 'infirmity of mind' in which there are two partial wills neither of which is 'entire' or 'whole'.[34]

---

34 Cook, *Alcohol*, p. 153. Victorinus is the philosopher whose con-version to Christianity Augustine took as the model for conversion, and whose path to Christianity he wished to follow himself.

At first glance this interpretation seems to describe a state of subjective internal conflict, the kind of experience that Paul presumably had in mind when praying to be delivered 'from this body of death'.[35] Further examination, however, reveals that such a simple argument fails to describe the situation adequately. What seems to be happening in the process of Augustine's thought has, Cook suggests, the character of dual volition, a phrase that he takes from Harry Frankfurt's discussion in *The Cambridge Companion to Augustine*.[36] On this understanding of the divided will, there are first-order volitional drives, which would mean for Augustine the wish to remain in his pagan way of life, and a second-order drive that urges him to turn away from his old ways and embrace Christianity. This is an important contribution to the background to Cook's theology in relation to addiction, because as he observes, Frankfurt himself uses the example of the addict to illustrate the problem he is addressing:

> For Frankfurt, the narcotic addict may have first-order desires both to take the drug and not to take it. The former is in both cases, more or less, generated by physiological dependency upon the drug. The 'unwilling addict', however, also has a second-order volition to stop taking the drug, and therefore identifies self with this first-order desire, while withdrawing from the first-order desire to stop using the drug.[37]

Cook then develops this idea in relation to 'salience' – the technical term for the way in which the use of a substance, or engagement in an activity such as gambling, can assume ever increasing importance in the life of the individual, and this salience conflicts with the volitional drive to abstain because of perceived 'psychological, social and biological harm associated with the dependent pattern of drug use'.[38] Putting this back

---

35 Romans 7.24.
36 Ed. Stump and Kretzmann, pp. 126–7.
37 Cook, *Alcohol*, p. 156.
38 Cook, *Alcohol*, p. 157.

into the language of Augustine, Cook quotes his view that 'the law of sin is the tyranny of habit, by which the mind is drawn and held even against its will. Yet it deserves to be so held because it so willingly falls into the habit.'[39]

Cook concludes by observing that although Augustine did not go into detail about the problems of alcohol excess, he did 'make it clear that drunkenness is a disorder of the will, consequent upon the sin of Adam', suggesting that the 'modern concepts of subjective compulsion, craving and addiction might be greatly illuminated by an application of this aspect of Augustine's thought'.[40]

Thomas Aquinas

In the ethical system of Thomas Aquinas, the key to understanding his writing in relation to addiction is to be found, Cook suggests, in his use of the 'mean of virtues' approach to Christian ethics. This presupposes a spectrum of views of the created order, at one end of which there is contempt for created things, which in its own way 'insults' the One who created everything, and at the other is excessive indulgence in the use of nature's goods. Between these two extremes there is the 'mean' – an attitude to created things that neither denies their goodness nor indulges in them to excess. Aquinas in the *Summa Theologica* uses the word 'temperance' to denote the right use of *reason* in making decisions about how to avoid the extremes. With regard to the application of this theory to the consumption of alcohol by an individual, Cook says:

> Notwithstanding the commendability of complete abstinence for those who choose it, the application of Aquinas' mean of virtues as an ethical framework to govern moderate drinking behaviour also has much to commend it. As a general rule, it would certainly seem that it is 'excessive' or heavy consumption that is associated with the greatest risk of harm,

39 Augustine, *Confessions* VIII, v, 12, cited in Cook, *Alcohol*, p. 157.
40 Cook, *Alcohol*, p. 59.

although there is a need to remember that the prevention paradox suggests that a moderate level of consumption alone will not solve all alcohol-related problems at the population level.[41]

Aquinas has a very helpful contribution to make to the study of addiction by his assertion that the appropriate use of God's creation, including alcohol, entails a positive valuation of things created and given to us, balanced by a *rational decision* to use such things in moderation – although that degree of moderation is not necessarily attainable by all.

Martin Luther

The Protestant reformer Martin Luther, like the Catholic Aquinas, concerns himself with reason as a guide to right thinking and right behaviour. He considers that states of drunkenness should rightly be regarded as 'a work of the flesh', something that is incompatible with the Christian virtuous life. Luther's moral code is based on a belief in the importance of following the Christian commandments as they are expressed in the Scriptures, so there is more to the Christian life than the conversion of the individual on the basis of faith; for faith has to be lived out through righteous behaviour, guided and enabled by the Holy Spirit – in every dimension of life, personal, communal and political.[42] He does not see Christian commitment as a guarantee of sinlessness, but attributes to the Holy Spirit a means of overcoming temptation. In some ways he tends, like Aquinas, towards a consequentialist view of drunkenness – being drunk when committing an evil act in no way excuses the individual from responsibility for what he has done while in this state of temporary 'diminished respon-

---

41 Cook, *Alcohol*, p. 176.

42 Perhaps the most recent outstanding example of this way of life being lived to the full can be found in the life, ministry, teaching and martyrdom of the Lutheran pastor Dietrich Bonhoeffer.

sibility'. In fact, quite the opposite conclusion is true. Cook quotes Luther himself on this:

> Is an offence, committed in a moment of intoxication, therefore excusable? Most assuredly not; on the contrary, drunkenness aggravates the fault ... This same drunkenness is a grievous vice among us Germans, and should be heavily chastised by the temporal magistrate, since the fear of God will not suffice to keep the brawling guzzlers in check.[43]

This highly important quotation not only illustrates Luther's awareness of excess as sinful in terms of behaviour, it establishes a link between God's rule and secular authority. The fear of God's wrath or punishment may not be enough to deter excess and its consequences, but fear of secular punishment may encourage moderation!

Luther's hostility to 'sins of the flesh' has strong backing in Scripture, particularly in Paul's wrestling with the concept of *flesh* in terms of his theology. However, it can be argued that Paul's use of the word 'flesh' carries a certain ambiguity of meaning, and care needs to be taken to avoid an unnecessary suggestion that there is a close relationship at all points between the words 'flesh' and 'evil'.

So Luther was aware not only of the tendency of human beings to drink too much alcohol but also of the social consequences of such excess, which cannot be excused by a plea of 'drunkenness', as if it were perhaps the fault of the alcohol that someone behaved wickedly. He therefore recommends rational moderation, and is sufficiently concerned about the extent of the problem to recommend that it should be a matter for legislation, and punishment for those who cannot control their consumption of alcohol without external constraint. He clearly does not advocate a policy of total abstention as a requisite for the Christian.

---

43 Martin Luther, *Table Talk: Of Offences*, paragraph 695, cited in Cook, *Alcohol*, p. 69.

Cook's ethical considerations

So how does Cook talk about the moral and immoral use and misuse of alcohol? From a theoretical point of view he does not explicitly identify his approach with any particular philosophical ethical framework. But he describes 'an interplay of agent and environment in such a way that subjects experience themselves as "drawn into" an addictive pattern of behaviour for which they are neither totally responsible nor entirely without responsibility'.[44] This approach is not perhaps easy to work with. It can be easier to adopt a 'take it or leave it' approach to ethics for religious thinkers, and it is greatly to his credit that Cook attempts to work in this more nuanced way, so that he cannot be accused of attempting to use religious language to close down the arguments, as is sometimes the case with more fundamentalist approaches. He also recognizes that although much of the ethical discourse, such as that of Aquinas, has been directed towards excess of alcohol consumption in view of its negative effect of drunkenness on society, there needs to be a counterbalancing emphasis on the *pursuit of the good as a positive goal*. For Christians this goal has to be located in the being and nature of God.

On the specifics of individual responsibility for the sensible consumption of alcohol, Cook identifies a number of helpful biblical texts. A passage from the apocryphal book of Sirach, for example, counsels the use of alcohol, but in moderation:

> Wine is very life to human beings if taken in moderation. What is life to one who is without wine? It has been created to make people happy. Wine drunk at the proper time and in moderation is rejoicing of heart and gladness of soul.[45]

There is, however, a following section which balances this liberal view by asserting that the excessive use of wine leads not to 'rejoicing' but to its opposite – 'bitterness of spirit, quarrels,

44 Cook, *Alcohol*, p. 146.
45 Sirach 31.25–31.

anger, and loss of strength'.[46] This and many other texts in both Jewish and New Testament Scriptures, notably in lists of vices and virtues (as can be found at Romans 13.13; Colossians 3.18—4.1; 1 Peter 4.3; 1 Timothy 3), warn us about the danger of excess, especially for members of the Christian ministry. Although all of these counsel sensible restraint in the use of alcohol, the practical wisdom of Sirach is of great importance as it presents the kind of balanced picture that occurs in later Christian theology – such as the 'mean of virtues' approach of Thomas Aquinas, who rejects the need for total abstinence because God's gifts are essentially good, but also opposes over-indulgence as it offends against the deadly sin of gluttony.

With regard to alcohol and public policy, corporate attempts to control both alcohol and drug misuse by the 'body politic' have a chequered history. On 2 March 2009 the devolved Scottish Parliament, in the face of alarming statistics,[47] decided to introduce, via taxation, a minimum price per unit of alcohol. Following much debate, from 1 May 2018 in Scotland there has been a pricing policy for alcoholic beverages set at a mini-mum of 50 pence per unit. In practice this means, for example, that a 70 cl bottle of whisky, which contains approximately 28 units of alcohol, will cost at least £14. There has been much opposition to this proposed legislation, including from the Scottish whisky industry and it is debatable what the charge per unit might achieve, except to penalize those who drink alcohol responsibly. People who wish to drink excessively will usually find the means of doing so no matter what this costs, including the cost incurred by society as a whole through traf-fic accidents and crime. At the same time, it is important to recognize that the number of alcohol-related deaths per year in the UK has been rising in recent years, so the makers of pub-lic policy are undoubtedly right to be concerned, and maybe doing nothing is no longer an option. We should distinguish

---

46 Cook, *Alcohol*, p. 39.

47 It was announced in the press that the number of alcohol-related admissions to hospital in Scotland in the previous year had risen to an all-time high of 1,500.

between alcohol excess and true addiction, however; addiction may not necessarily involve great amounts on a daily basis, but reflects a state of pathological dependency.

Cook looks at public responses to the problems of alcohol-related violence, disease and trauma in his chapter entitled 'Alcohol, addiction and Christian ethics'. He regards this aspect of ethical concern as of great importance, although he seems, justifiably perhaps, somewhat pessimistic about how far such policies and their implementation can go towards finding a solution to the misuse of alcohol. Cook addresses the problem of collusion between the government and alcohol-producing companies. There can be an element of hubris in the responses from official bodies, including the government. The government claims to want people to use alcohol responsibly, and suggests setting a rate of taxation based partly on 'units'; but it also benefits greatly from tax on alcoholic beverages, so there can be a conflict of interest at work here.

This is one of Cook's most important insights because of its engagement not only with aspects of *personal morality* in relation to alcohol consumption but with the *perceived duty of national governments* to find ways of tackling the medical, social and criminal problems associated with excess. As Cook correctly points out, however:

> the balancing of health concerns against the benefits of alcohol in society will never be an easy matter while health is merely set against the pleasures which some associate with alcohol. A point of reference is required which lies beyond profit, and even beyond health and pleasure.[48]

Cook identifies a number of highly significant elements in the story of alcohol and its misuse, including attempts by both church and state to deal with the problems this has caused over the last hundred years, from the work of the temperance movement to the considerable amount of attention paid by governments to the idea that changing the law can be an effec-

---

48 Cook, *Alcohol*, p. 191.

tive instrument of harm reduction. He is sceptical about how far this will work, not least because both the alcohol industry and governments are concerned not only with public health and social cohesion but also with maximizing revenue.

Conclusion

Looking at the theological writing on addiction, it is obvious that some questions remain unanswered. For May, we are all attached to something, so by extension we are all addicts: this view seems to me to be in danger of reducing the concept of addiction to meaninglessness. For Nelson and his 'AA' approach, those who are alcoholics (such as himself) will always be in the process of recovery, a view rejected by many in the healthcare professions. In Cook's writing we find a concentration on the disease element in substance dependency, balanced by a concern with personal and public morality in the light of Christian teaching down through the ages. He tends to see the appropriateness of the use of alcohol as circumstantial.

What emerges from these arguably unsatisfactory or contradictory statements about addiction is the need for a new way of understanding the causes of addiction, and more importantly the best way of helping addicted people. Can we discover a 'new model' that promises a more effective methodology for offering pastoral help to those who are substance dependent? The new model I am proposing begins with *human desire*. What are the positive desires, longings and aspirations that motivate human beings? And how can such desires be properly housed within the worshipping life and fellowship of the Christian Church? The answers to these questions lie in an exploration of the theology of desire as addressed by some of the most important writers on this subject, with particular emphasis on how their ideas may be linked with the phenomenon of addiction.

3

The Theological Understanding
of Desire

Paul and freedom

Desire plays a most important role in the understanding of
what happens when an individual becomes addicted to something. Whether we are thinking about substance dependency on
alcohol or drugs of various kinds, or activities such as gambling,
this desire factor is always involved. To use the vocabulary of
the healthcare psychologist Jim Orford, it is helpful to think
of addiction as 'excessive desire', or even more specifically
as 'uncontrollable desire'. Both these definitions concentrate
on human appetites for things: but it is obvious that desire
can be good or bad, depending on what I desire, and in what
amount. I want to eat, because without experiencing hunger I
would not eat, and that would, over time, inevitably destroy
my health. But excessive desire, particularly for things such as
alcohol, can gradually undermine the functioning of parts of
the human body, such as the liver, the heart, and ultimately the
brain. The misuse of other drugs such as cocaine or heroin can
also have a disastrous effect on people's human relationships,
at many levels, and on their relationship with God.

This raises the question of how we determine, from a
religious point of view, what makes the human desires, and
their satisfaction, a good or bad thing. It also invites us to try
to understand the conflict we can experience between the wish
to follow God's will and the opposite attraction – to behave
exactly as we please, however damaging such actions may be
to our physical and mental health, and to our family life.

The earliest Christian worshipping communities had to deal with these questions as part of their everyday attempts to live out their Christian vocation in an ethical way. And it is clear that some communities often found it hard to discern, or live up to, the ideals of the Church as described in the New Testament. In 1 Corinthians 11, for example, Paul finds it necessary to criticize the lifestyle of some members who are inclined to overindulge in both food and wine at the church meetings for worship. There is a suggestion here that part of the problem was that some members were left to starve while others ate and drank to excess, which suggested a lack of proper loving concern for one another.

And in some of the 'household codes' for Christian behaviour there is a specific concern for sobriety in family life. In 1 Timothy 3 we find instructions for bishops, deacons and their families, that commend a restrained approach to the taking of wine – perhaps this indicates that the writer of the pastoral letters had experience of churches where alcoholic excess had caused problems.

What we are working towards here is the legitimate expression of human desire within the context of a Christian worshipping community. This leads us to a brief consideration of three major themes that Paul considers in his letters: *inner conflict*, *freedom* and *grace*.

Inner conflict

With regard to *conflict*, the key passage is the consideration of human motivation that Paul talks about in Romans 7. From the time of Augustine onwards, and emphasized also by Martin Luther at the time of the Reformation, there has been a belief that this chapter should be interpreted in a literal sense, as an interior debate about what we ought to do, what we ought not to do, and the difficulty we all seem to experience at times about doing what we believe to be God's will for us.[1]

---

1 This view was, however, challenged by Krister Stendahl in his book *Paul among Jews and Gentiles* in the 1970s.

If we accept that this interpretation is basically correct, then what is going on here? Why can it be so hard for us to behave in a way that is consistent with what we claim to believe as Christians? Many writers have tried to get at what Paul is saying. Taken at face value, it is fairly obvious, as many of us do at times find it hard to behave in accordance with our conscience. And the person dependent on drugs or alcohol is a particularly good example of this; people who experience this kind of personal struggle often speak of their bafflement about why they find it so hard to give up their self-destructive activity. But Paul is suggesting that an *almost personalized idea of sin* is the problem – sin can somehow interfere either with our understanding of what is good and proper with regard to desire, or with our ability to overcome our temptation to do what we believe to be wrong. This suggestion does not solve all the problems, but it can be seen as a charitable, rather than a judgemental, view. If the problem originates in 'sin' in this external, personalized way, then perhaps we human beings have only a partial responsibility for the damage it can do to our lives – and perhaps also a proportionate responsibility to look for help when we find the journey out of slavery to sin very long and difficult.

We can also, however, look at this dilemma about human desire through the eyes of the New Testament scholar Gerd Theissen, who in his book *Psychological Aspects of Pauline Theology* imaginatively weaves ideas about the divided self from his understanding of both New Testament theology and modern psychology.

Theissen sets up what he describes as a 'three tribunal' approach to psychological conflict. There is the individual, standing halfway between two sets of competing desires. On the one hand there is the possibility of choosing to do what is believed to be God's will; on the other is the possibility of choosing what we know to be against this. In the case of the addicted person, this is the choice between continuing in the addicted state or choosing the path of sobriety. That is the choice viewed from a spiritual perspective.

On the psychological aspect of this, Theissen relates it to Sigmund Freud's picture of the human mind as having three 'compartments' which are often in conflict with one another almost from the moment we are born. The *superego* represents one tribunal in its demands that we behave according to an internalized pattern of behaviour that is laid down by others – parents, teachers, clergy or 'society'. The *id* represents a second tribunal – a chaotic, desire-driven set of motivations without regard for any moral considerations or legal systems. The *ego*, the third tribunal, describes the place where 'reason and common sense' stands between them, being constantly pulled in two opposite directions, often below the level of conscious awareness.[2] It is the conflict set up in this way by the mind that explains, from a psychological point of view, the painful conflict faced by every addict – no matter what the cause of the addiction may seem to be.

Freedom

Freedom is one of the most important of the fundamental ideas about desire as Paul presents them. So what is the problem that he faces? The Christian, Paul tells us on many occasions, has been liberated from Jewish law. In fact, as many New Testament commentators suggest, the Jewish law, which was the way of life previously followed by all the Jewish members of the Christian Church, is almost equated with sinfulness for the Christian who tries to incorporate it into the Christian way of life. Its 'boundary markers', such as circumcision of males, and rules about what to eat, can play no valid part in the life of the Christian; it is out of the question to try to force them on church members who do not come from a Jewish background (as a rite of admission to Christian church membership, for example), as the letter to the Galatians makes quite clear.

Alongside this, there was a complementary belief that because we belong to the Body of Christ, and because of our

---

2 Charles Rycroft, *A Critical Dictionary of Psychoanalysis*.

reception of the Holy Spirit, we are enabled to live in the freedom of the Spirit, without concerning ourselves with minute rules and regulations about how to live our daily lives. We will be guided by the Spirit of the risen Saviour, and that is all that matters. So just as the Jewish *rituals* could be discarded, so too the *moral aspects of the same law* were now irrelevant for the Christian believer. That is how many of the Christians in churches that Paul knew personally interpreted the message.

But Paul was opposed to the view that individuals who had been converted could behave in any way they choose, attributing this supposed freedom to the guidance of the Spirit. Paul sees the Church as a community of people who have to live their lives in a way that has a moral foundation, otherwise their lives will be chaotic, and the Church divided. There is, at the heart of Christianity, a commandment to love, to be genuinely concerned not only for one's own well-being but for that of the whole Church. The idea of freedom has to be held in balance with this vision of mutual love and concern. The practical aspects of this part of Paul's teaching can be found in many passages, but it is summed up excellently in the famous 'Hymn to Charity' found in 1 Corinthians 13. This message does not deny the idea of human freedom in the Spirit, but insists that it has to be held in tension with the commandment to love one another, without relying on the keeping of the law to achieve salvation. And the various New Testament 'household codes'[3] give practical guidance as to how the Christian should behave – at the heart of this there is an 'imperative based on an indicative': because Christ has done so much for us, this is how we should treat each other in response to his gifts to us.

This is highly important as we try to design a pastoral approach to the needs of people addicted to drugs and alcohol. Our aim is to offer people in these situations hope for the future, hope that is based on a positive desire for a better lifestyle, free from the imprisonment that drugs can impose on our

---

3 See, for example, Colossians 3.18–24.

lives. In this context, one goal may well be to help the addicted person to see his use of a drug not as the exercise of *freedom* but as a form of *slavery to a substance*. For Paul, there is a form of slavery that is truly to be welcomed, but that is 'slavery' to Jesus Christ, and even to one another: he tells us that as Christians we have exchanged slavery to unnecessary rules and regulations for slavery to Christ, and this is the true basis of freedom. So in 1 Corinthians 7.22 Paul argues that 'he who was called in the Lord as a slave is a freedman of the Lord. Likewise he who was free when called is a slave of Christ.' The practical obligations of this are spelled out in detail by Paul in Galatians 5.22–24, having just told the congregation, 'through love be servants of one another'. So freedom allows for the expression of desire, but this must, for the Christian, be balanced by mutual love and responsibility.

Grace

At the intersection of life as it is with all its limitations, and life as it can become under God's guidance and power, comes the concept of grace. For Gerald May, divine grace, an unmerited free gift from a loving heavenly Father, is the spiritual key to release from addiction, whether to substances or to life-limiting behaviours, including the *compulsive* need for receiving the praise of other people. This clearly echoes Paul's belief that when we are converted to the Christian faith and baptized into the worshipping community we are placed on a new footing in terms of our relationship with God – and the foremost concept here is undoubtedly grace. So what does this somewhat elusive word mean?

Grace enables individuals to live according to God's commandments, as interpreted by Jesus Christ; it also helps us to live as part of a community that has mutual responsibilities. And this enabling grace is expressed actively in Christian congregations in many ways, including the various 'charisms' of the Church – in differing forms of ministry, for example, as set out in 1 Corinthians 12. And God's grace, freely given and thankfully received, also 'breeds' grace in response to its reception. One concrete example of this 'chain reaction' was the willingness of the Christians in Corinth to make a significant financial contribution to Jerusalem-based Christians who were in desperate need. The most powerful witness to the reception of grace is when those who have received it become 'a vehicle of that same grace to others'. And as a highly relevant footnote to that very important idea in terms of addiction and its treatment, it is often men and women who have themselves been through a time of addiction who are best suited to give vital help and encouragement to others who are still on that journey.

Those of us who provide pastoral and spiritual guidance to people with addictions will probably find that grace, enabling grace as described by Paul, can be of great help. It can be accessed in many ways, not least through prayer and the Christian sacraments, particularly Holy Communion and anointing. There is nothing magical about these sacramental interventions, but they are signs of God's grace entering that person's life through our ministry, combined with prayer and attentive listening – and the capacity to wait for things to change, which will often involve time, effort and a lot of patience.

At the heart of much of what I have been saying concerning Paul's theology is the question of desire and how desire can be best experienced and expressed in a Christian church. Many issues, including questions about sexuality, are part of that process of theological discernment, some of which can cause division and argument within church communities. The use and misuse of alcohol and drugs is one element in this discernment process. Sometimes no clear or universally accepted rules can be applied, particularly with regard to alcohol. But the concern about what is good and edifying for the whole community is highly important here, as we saw in relation to the greed and drunkenness of Christians in their worship meals at Corinth. Individual communities have to work out for themselves what truly builds community and what may be destructive, and what can be done for individuals in that community when things go wrong.

Augustine – desire and the divided self

Augustine of Hippo is an equally important source of thinking on the subject of human desires. The question here has to do with desire – in the sense of *asking what desires are of ultimate importance to the Christian*, and then finding out how that can influence other lesser desires.

In thinking about addiction from the starting point of what we might call 'legitimate' and 'excessive or inappropriate' desires, Augustine can give us some important clues in our attempt to provide pastoral and spiritual care. In the opening lines of the first chapter of his great spiritual autobiography, the *Confessions*, he makes it clear that for human beings there is a restlessness of the soul that only finds relief and new purposefulness in a relationship with God. The quotation is well known – 'You stir man to take pleasure in praising you, because you have made us for yourself, and our heart is restless until it rests in you.'[4] As suggested earlier, questions about human desires are fundamental to the care of addicted people and Augustine provides a map for this by placing desire for God at the apex of human longing – every other wish, aspiration or desire, every human longing, will only lead to fulfilment if we begin from that starting point. This is a total, uncompromising attitude, but it is not necessarily to be seen as harsh or puritanical in its intention.

It is perhaps tempting at times to view Augustine as being opposed to the taking of pleasure, whether in eating and drinking or in sexual activity. His conversion to Christianity as an adult led him to review every aspect of his earlier life, including his relationship with a woman which had led to the birth

---

4 As Henry Chadwick points out in his translation of the *Confessions*, this quotation 'announces a major theme of his work'.

of his son Adeodatus. But to view the Christian Augustine in this rather narrow or pleasure-forbidding manner does not do justice to the complexity of his thoughts about 'the flesh', which he undoubtedly saw as having a close and indestructible relationship with the human spirit. In one of his collected Letters (no. 140) he writes:

> So great a power does the sweet companionship of the flesh and soul have! *For no one ever hates his own flesh* (Eph. 5:29), and for this reason the soul also does not want to leave its weakness even for a time, though it trusts that it will receive its flesh for eternity without weakness.

So for Augustine there was an entirely appropriate relationship – a 'sweet companionship' – between the body and the soul. But this relationship has to be directed in a spiritually wholesome and positive way.

What Augustine tries to do in his discussion of the use we make of creation is to see created things as having two aspects: the thing itself – food, drink, enjoyment of all created things, including human relationships – and the deeper, spiritual reality that such things point towards. What he comes to see is that although we are allowed by God to find enjoyment in created things, they can become a distraction from ultimate joy when we fail to see beyond the created objects themselves. Instead we should be aware of their true importance, leading us imaginatively towards the God by whom they are created, and towards whom the whole of our lives should be oriented.

In his writings on Christian teaching, Augustine makes use of two Latin verbs: *uti*, meaning to make use of something but at the same time to see beyond it to God, and *frui*, which refers to the enjoyment we get from using things without necessarily seeing beyond their immediate enjoyment. Thinking about this in relation to addiction, the difference between these two words becomes clear. If we drink alcohol, for example, to experience the flavour of a good wine, to enjoy the pleasant sensation it produces, or to drink it in company with others at a meal, there is in principle nothing wrong with this. But if we reach a point where the alcohol produces a euphoric state of being, or is used to combat uncomfortable thoughts or feelings, then we are using alcohol in a way that can be destructive. We are using alcohol not to enhance our lives and to give praise to God our creator, but as an escape from what is most real and in our own best interests. And Augustine knew that his mother Monica had at one time in her life been subject to a 'foul addiction' to alcohol, as he mentions in the *Confessions*, so he was speaking from personal experience of someone very close to him.

What he is telling us is that there is a world of difference, from a religious or spiritual point of view, between enjoying things for their own sake and enjoying them as things that point beyond themselves; they become, to use his language, 'signs' pointing to the ultimate reality, the ultimate enjoyment of life, which can only be found in God himself. So he is advising us as Christians not to avoid the pleasures of life, of what God has created, but to recognize in those things a route to encountering God, which is the only possible way to true and lasting happiness.[5]

Augustine recognized that the best human endeavours are often sabotaged by internal conflict – what he describes as a *divided will*. On the one hand we wish to do what we believe to be good and virtuous things, and on the other we encounter the reality of desires that oppose this. This echoes to some extent Paul's cry of anguish in Romans 7, deploring the fact that often we do things that we believe to be wrong, and expressing a longing to be delivered from this demoralizing conflict, 'this body of death'.

It was clear to Augustine that his life before his conversion to Christianity had been one of prolonged internal conflict. The *Confessions* make this clear. He had enjoyed his life outside the Christian Church, with the freedom he found in his family

---

5 This aspect of Augustine's thought can be followed up in his book *De Doctrina Christiana*, translated into English as *Teaching Christianity*.

life and as a teacher of rhetoric. But there was a spiritual rest-lessness that came from deep in his psyche, and also through the examples provided by the lives of others he admired, and in a sense wanted to copy. Most important of these people from the beginning of his life was his mother Monica; later on he was much influenced by the greatest theologian of his day, Ambrose, and a good friend whose name was Victorinus. These all helped by their example and teaching to set him firmly on the road to Christian orthodoxy. He also records in the *Confessions* that he had begun to find the teachings of the Manichean religion, which he had for a while embraced, intellectually unsatisfying.

It is clear that this dissatisfaction led Augustine, via much soul-searching, to the moment of decision. A real conflict of the will accompanied this decision-making. He was torn between remaining in his pagan lifestyle, and submitting to the Christian Church. He describes that conflict in detail in his writings.

As this is so fundamental to the issues of addiction it is worth trying to understand this kind of conflict in more depth. Addicted people often recognize their difficulties when they attempt to give up their alcohol or drug dependencies. There is a deep-seated conflict between the wish to give up what they know is a harmful activity and the wish to continue it, and it is this conflict that can make addiction so hard, or impossible, to overcome.

One of the best descriptions of the psychological aspects of the divided will can be found in *The Cambridge Companion to Augustine*, in a chapter by Eleonore Stump.[6] The root of the problem is to be found in the idea of primary and second-ary volition (the word *desire* is roughly equivalent to *volition*). Stump explains that a person first forms a primary volition – the will to 'directing some faculty or bodily power to do something' – and then a second-order volition – 'the will to will something'. The example she gives is forming the will

6 See pp. 126ff. There is also a very helpful detailed discussion of this in Cook, *Alcohol*.

to avoid eating meat. The trouble is that the determination to do such a thing is not always successful, which is the problem that Augustine faced. He knew that his will to do things was compromised by other wishes or desires, and that people can, to use Stump's terminology, 'violate the rules that they have set for themselves'. The question is – why does this happen? The argument here is about the freedom of the will – it raises issues about how far our actions are determined and how far we are able to choose them. Again we hear an echo of Paul: 'For I do not do what I want, but I do the very thing that I hate.'

Augustine wrote extensively about this question, so how did he resolve it? The discussions of first- and second-order volitions are philosophically highly complex and seem to raise as many questions as they answer. But the conclusion we may come to on the basis of this discussion can be simplified in relation to addiction. Christopher Cook, writing about addiction as sin and syndrome, makes the point that for Augustine the fundamental question remains one of directing desire towards various objectives. These can be summed up, he suggests, in terms of this question: 'Will life be fulfilled by striving for the highest good, or will it be subject to concupiscence, and thus be characterized by a divided, captive will?' And he concludes by saying that 'for Augustine, the solution to this dilemma was to be found in the grace of God, which alone provided a route to freedom'.[7] From a pastoral point of view, our efforts to help addicted people will inevitably involve the process of finding ways of making that enabling grace available to them.

In Augustine's thought there is a clear distinction between using created things – food, wine, sex – for the pleasure they provide and for the way in which they point beyond themselves to God. He sometimes goes to extremes in this, suggesting that eating food is rather like taking medication, something necessary for us but not really to be enjoyed for its own sake. And with regard to sexual activity he argues, unsurprisingly, that to take pleasure in sexual acts without the possibility of

---

7 See Cook, *Alcohol*, p. 161.

conception is a misuse of sexuality – so at times his writing can seem rather bleak.

But we need to go beyond his immediate ideas to find out more about what he is really arguing. Any serious reading of the *Confessions* will make it clear that for the mature Augustine the ultimate desire, the ultimate pleasure in living, comes from a deep and lasting relationship with God, the God who has made us for himself and without whose presence in our lives at all times we can only experience restlessness, spiritual and moral disorder and chaos. All human pursuit of ordinary desires must therefore be secondary to the pursuit of that relationship with God in order for life to be free, creative and fulfilling, both in this present lifetime and in eternity. 'Foul addictions' such as those to alcohol and illicit drugs can only damage that quest.

In my experience of working with people who are trying to conquer their addictions, I find that what Augustine is saying opens a very important door into the best way forward. Although it may be helpful, at some stage, to try to determine why an individual has become substance dependent, and even allowing for the many aspects of this traumatic experience that are likely to vary from person to person, it is in my estimation the process of striving for a worthwhile goal in life that is most beneficial for the sufferer both now and in the future. A setting of new goals that are genuinely in the best interests of the person may be particularly effective in achieving this, with the right help and lasting support of others, whether in clinical practice, psychotherapy, or in the task of pastoral counselling.

In terms of spiritual guidance, as Christian pastors we are concerned to help all the people we encounter to find their way to a mature and profound relationship with God as revealed in the person of Jesus Christ. This is the point at which our work will inevitably differ from that of other professions such as psychotherapy or social work; these may or may not refer to religious ideas in their work, but that is not likely to be their main focus. So when we are working with addicted people who are trying to change their lives for the better, it may very well be that in addition to helping them towards setting new goals and aspirations for their lives, we will be trying to help them – as a matter of priority and urgency – to discover the grace that comes from a life lived in the light of spiritual awareness, assisted by prayer and the sacraments.

Before leaving the theological ideas and moving on to specific pastoral considerations, it may be helpful to refer to a way of thinking that tries to make sense of the idea of inner conflict by addressing theological and psychological points of view side by side.

The best introduction to this is probably the work of Léon Turner in his book *Theology, Psychology and the Plural Self*. Writing from both psychological and theological points of view he explains inner conflict by suggesting, in line with many contemporary psychologists, that it is a mistake to think of personality as unified, and unchanging over the years. Instead, it is more likely that all human beings have a number of co-existing 'plastic' sub-personalities that all function together deep within us, and change over time. And this is not to suggest that these sub-personalities are bound to be competing with each other in a *pathological* way; rather we call upon aspects of them to help and guide us in a variety of social situations. But this *can* cause inner conflicts, and this may well be at the heart of addiction, when two elements of our personalities – the wish to drink excessively or to use drugs in a harmful way, and the wish to give these things up – find themselves in competition.

It is also helpful to recognize that although desire is a perfectly normal human experience, there are times when desire has to be educated – or re-educated – for the sake of individuals and communities and even whole societies. This is the approach that Timothy Gorringe takes in his book *The Education of Desire*. He comments on the way that our contemporary world often seems to set in front of us goals of how to live that are dictated not by spiritual values – in the widest sense – as much as by the wish of large multinational companies to make a profit from selling us their produce, thereby subtly suggesting that consumerism is the way to happiness. The addicted person may have lost the ability to make this kind of distinction, and if so our spiritual and pastoral ministry may involve helping them to restructure their personal values and aspirations. It is often the case that our thoughts and imagination are influenced in ways that we are not aware of by things like high-powered advertising campaigns for products that, it is subliminally suggested, will enhance our appearance or make us more obviously attractive to other people in a variety of ways. The re-education of desire, then, will have the task of showing these things to be essentially worthless, and encouraging us to look for more reliable ways of relating to others both professionally and socially. There is a clear spiritual component to this – the enhancement of our selves through consumerism can generate a false self, in contrast to the spiritual gospel with its insistence that it is the truth that will really set us free.

Desire has an ambiguous role for the Christian. It can direct us towards actions that are entirely consistent with our understanding of God's will both for ourselves and for the church community that we belong to – and even, in a wider sense, for the society of which we are part. But it can also lead us in the opposite direction, in ways that are destructive of our health and of our commitments and responsibilities. In Paul's words, 'All things are lawful for me, but not all things are helpful ... All things are lawful, but not all things build up.'[8] For the alcoholic or drug addict, a point can be reached where considerations of health and social well-being at every level are severely compromised. In these circumstances, the pastor's work will be to help the affected individual towards a new understanding of his priorities and aspirations, with a view to understanding the role – particularly the negative role – played by the addiction in relation to those positive desires.

---

8 1 Corinthians 6.12; 10.23.

4

The Pastoral Care of People with Addictions

It is now time to look in detail at the pastoral care of addicted people. This chapter begins with a carefully constructed discussion of how to determine whether an individual is just a user of one or more substances, or whether he is really addicted, and then considers in detail Richard Osmer's model of pastoral care with its four phases. Some practical suggestions are offered about safety and security for addicts and those who help them, and this is followed by a brief description of the current picture of substance addiction in the UK. I then introduce my aspirational model of pastoral care, which can be adapted for use with people who are addicted to substance use.

Identifying addiction

How can we know for certain whether a person is really addicted to the use of alcohol or another substance such as heroin? This is a very important subject to address, because many people make use of these things on a regular basis without showing any of the recognized symptoms of addiction. A regular or even heavy drinker is not necessarily an alcoholic.

One of the most distinguished experts on this subject, Griffith Edwards, for many years a consultant at the Maudsley Psychiatric Hospital in London and a professor at the Institute of Psychiatry, produced a very helpful checklist of addiction symptoms in his book *Matters of Substance*. I use his model as a guide to this process of discernment.

Edwards identifies seven symptoms of addiction, and suggests that when several of these are present in a particular individual the word addict may well be appropriate.

- *The subjective awareness of a changed relationship with a drug*
  He mentions as an example the typical alcoholic's frank admission at an AA meeting that alcohol has become the controlling factor in her life: this moment of honesty may come after many months, or even years, of denial of the condition to oneself and to others – family, colleagues, friends and so on. It is what James Nelson in his book *Thirst* refers to as the 'oops phenomenon' – the point at which for one reason or another, an alcoholic recognizes and accepts that she is 'hooked'.

- *An acquired brain tolerance to the drug's effects*
  The same amount of a drug will have a progressively reduced effect on the substance-dependent person than on an ordinary user because of changes in the chemistry of the brain in response to significant and long-term substance use. Because of this physiological dimension I entirely agree with those clinicians who argue that tolerance is one of the two principal determining symptoms of addiction (the other being withdrawal symptoms, see below).

- *Withdrawal symptoms*
  These can range from mild shakiness to serious, even life-threatening fits and delirium tremens, which is why it is necessary for a long-term drinker to have his withdrawal managed properly. It is tempting to tell a chronically dependent drinker to just stop drinking. Although this is likely to be well meant, it is actually dangerous for someone who is drinking vastly more than the recommended allowance of alcohol to stop abruptly.

- *Taking the drug to relieve the withdrawal symptoms*
  This is fairly obvious – the hangover (or worse) can be temporarily relieved by going back to the same drug. But this pattern is problematic over time partly because of the acquired tolerance factor mentioned above.

- *Increased salience of the need for the drug over competing needs and responsibilities*
  Most people enjoy a range of activities related to work or leisure, but for the true addict this range shrinks in the direction of spending more time and effort on acquiring and using the drug of choice. This salience factor can include the misuse of money needed for essentials such as paying rent and buying food. It is also the case that many drug users gradually lose interest in normal socialization or spending time with their family and children, and do not engage in ordinary pastimes such as sporting activity or going to films, concerts or theatres.

- *Narrowing of the drug-taking repertoire*
  The drug use gradually becomes mechanical and repetitive, rather than something that happens at certain specific times of the day, such as drinking some wine with a meal.

- *Reinstatement after abstinence*
  When a person has managed to be sober and abstinent for a substantial period of time but then goes back to the drug of choice, she will very quickly return to the same level of use as she was taking before quitting – *because the brain remembers how much she used to take*, and tries to get back to that level as quickly as possible.

Griffith Edwards says that when we see a person exhibiting some or all of these symptoms, then we may well conclude that he or she has, or is developing, an addictive lifestyle relative to a drug or activity. I find this list very helpful in trying to determine whether someone is occasionally overindulgent or truly dependent on the drug or activity in question.

Richard Osmer's four phases of pastoral care

At this point it will be useful to look at a model of pastoral care that can be adapted where necessary to address the circumstances of people with substance misuse problems. This is the excellent overview of Christian pastoral care by the American theologian Richard Osmer: *Practical Theology*. Osmer breaks down the process of pastoral care into four phases:

1 What is going on? This is the *descriptive-empirical task*, involving information gathering about a particular situation.
2 Why is this going on? This *interpretive task* phase looks at the 'patterns and dynamics' of a particular situation, and uses ideas from a wide range of disciplines as necessary to understand it better.
3 What ought to be going on? Osmer calls this the *normative task*, in which theological concepts and ethical ideas are brought into the picture to help in the interpretive process.
4 Finally, the *pragmatic task* – this is the strategic approach to the problem, the attempt to 'influence situations in ways that are desirable', and monitoring what happens in response to such initiatives.

How can these four stages of pastoral insight and intervention help the Christian minister to provide a helpful engagement with people who are addicted to alcohol or drugs, or both, and their families and others in their social environment?

What is going on?

The first task is uncontroversial. Without an accurate understanding of the situation, the pastor cannot hope to make a positive contribution to the problems faced by a person who is dependent on drugs. But here we immediately meet a frequent difficulty, because people who are substance dependent very often deny their addiction, and try to hide the evidence of what they are doing. That deception may be part of the individual's own defensive self-image – what Gerald May in *Addiction and Grace* calls the 'I can handle it' ploy. Someone I knew used to boast about his large alcohol intake, which eventually destroyed his liver. He seemed to have little or no awareness that he was an alcoholic, and his family consistently colluded with this denial. It is a short step from denying the addiction to *oneself* to denying it to *others* – family, friends, doctors, clergy, and in some circumstances the police and other statutory authorities.

How can we approach this denial factor effectively? Two practical suggestions by Osmer are helpful here. The first is the importance of engaging informally in conversation with the addicted person's friends and family to get a clearer picture of what is really happening. These conversations are partly an acknowledgement of the needs of the family as a whole in relation to the addicted individual, and must, of course, be undertaken with great sensitivity and discretion. But in our contemporary church *issues of safeguarding are of great importance*, and we may need to involve church safeguarding officers if others, particularly children, are believed to be at risk. This requirement can sometimes override issues of confidentiality. Second, it is often productive to pay attention to the addicted person's feelings, which may be conveyed as much through body language as through his words. It's what Osmer calls listening with a 'third ear' to what the person is saying. All this can help the pastor to break through the barriers of silence and deception, and get to know the situation as it really is, bearing in mind that others besides the addicted person may have an investment in withholding the truth; they may feel ashamed because of these addictions, and the Christian pastor may (no doubt wrongly) be seen as a judgemental figure, in contrast perhaps to a local doctor.

Why is this going on?

The second, interpretive, task is perhaps the most difficult in relation to addiction, because there can be so many reasons why people become overdependent on drugs of one kind or another. Any number of factors can propel people into a potentially destructive use of alcohol, or drugs such as heroin, cocaine or their derivatives. Many people use them to try to cope with emotional problems such as depression or anxiety. The trouble with this is that the drug in question can only temporarily mask uncomfortable emotional states, it can't cure them: and the 'tolerance' factor means that it is likely that increasing amounts of the drug will be gradually needed to produce the same amount of relief. In some cases we should encourage the person experiencing psychological problems such as depression to get medical help in the form of pharmacological or psychological therapy, or both.

It is likely that these elements of psychological or emotional distress will be linked to the circumstances of a person's life. Life-changing incidents such as the loss of a job, the loss of a partner through death or divorce, or the loss of one's home can push *some* people towards the misuse of drugs, including alcohol. And if two or more distressing events happen close together, there is the risk that this accumulation of challenging events will lead to an increasing dependency on drugs or alcohol – or both. The person who reacts in this way to stressful incidents in life frequently enters a downward spiral of increasing dependency. The use of non-prescription drugs as a form of psychological pain relief does nothing to address the underlying problems for the user: if anything, it is likely to make them worse. As pastors we should remember that the use of a substance may well indicate some form of underlying distress related to disturbing life events: in these circumstances we should attend to that painful experience rather than just seeing the substance-dependency problem in isolation.

What ought to be going on?

When we come to the third stage, what Osmer calls the *normative task*, we begin to engage with specifically religious ideas and concepts. The Christian Church tries to understand human desires, for food, drink, intimacy and other desirable things, in the context of Christian discipleship and witness. One important element here is the recognition that the availability, affordability and social acceptance of alcohol are significant factors. I am not necessarily arguing for a policy of total abstinence for the Christian (as in other faiths such as Islam) but for a methodology for determining what level of consumption of alcohol and other drugs is compatible with a Christian lifestyle. It may, however, be very difficult to generalize about this. No doubt various denominations and church communities will find opportunities to discuss these issues and form a judgement about them on a local basis. As with many ethical issues, these conversations themselves, reflecting a variety of points of view, are probably the most important thing, even though we may hope to reach a consensus.

As a further reflection on the ethical elements of this, we would do well to recall the warning that Christopher Cook puts forward in *Alcohol, Addiction and Christian Ethics*, that governments, not least in the UK, obtain very large tax revenues from the sale of alcohol, which may produce a conflict of interest when governments get involved in the debate about excessive drinking, and suggest introducing minimum pricing according to the number of units of alcohol being consumed.

The strategic approach

The fourth stage in the pastoral response in general, and relating to addicted people in particular is the *pragmatic task*. This involves the pastor's personal engagement with a particular situation, whether it concerns people who are ill, a family problem, the loss of someone's job, or ministry at the time of a death. It may also involve ministry to people who are affected by addictions – the addicted person himself, his partner, children, other family members, friends or colleagues. As suggested earlier in relation to the writings of Kenneth Leech, we must not assume too easily that the addiction factor necessarily makes a lot of difference to the way in which we approach an individual – we are still ministering to a person, and the nature of their difficulty may well be similar in some respects to those encountered by people facing other challenging situations. Leech has a great deal to say about the ways in which addiction, particularly to some 'hard' drugs, introduces what may seem a strange, mysterious, in a way alien, element if we are not used to working with people in this kind of situation. So he advocates the acceptance of 'silence, darkness, and the way of unknowing' in the face of something that involves 'the pain, the wounds, the brokenness, the repeated crises and the darkness' that we will probably encounter in this kind of ministry.[1] There is much scope for sacramental ministry here, particularly through the Eucharist and the anointing of the sufferer with prayer and the laying on of hands. Much of this will depend on the degree of self-awareness of the addicted person, and part of our pastoral role may relate to the process of gradually and patiently helping individuals to reach the point of acceptance of the true nature of their addiction. Sadly, though, not all who suffer in this way come to that moment of enlightened self-knowledge.

Suggestions about safety and security

Who is at risk in the pastoral encounter between pastor and addict? It is possible to overestimate the danger of meeting with people who have become addicted to drugs or alcohol. In reality, people who come looking for help are generally at a very low point in their personal journey through life – few of us look for help unless we are feeling pretty desperate!

---

1 Quoted by Bunch and Ritchie in *Prayer and Prophecy. The Essential Kenneth Leech*, p. 140.

On the other hand, clergy, usually those living in areas of social deprivation, have often felt threatened in their homes, either by the sheer numbers of people who come to the clergy home wanting help, or by the manner in which people present themselves. Clergy may also have experienced a sense of puzzlement about how best to help those who come to them. Fortunately the number of cases of clergy being attacked at home is low; but there is always a risk, and we have a right to protect ourselves, our families, homes and property.

Everyone involved is vulnerable in some way – the addict, their friends and family, and those who offer help.

The addict

It is worth stating again that the most vulnerable person in the room is almost certainly the person with the addiction. I'm reminded of Lewis Carroll's conversation between the King of Hearts and the Hatter in *Alice in Wonderland*:

> King: If that's all you know about it you may stand down.
> Hatter: I ca'n't go no lower, I'm on the floor as it is.

Or, to quote John Bunyan: 'He that is down need fear no fall; He that is low, no pride.'

The alcoholic or the drug misuser is often very much like the Hatter in *Alice* – very nearly at rock bottom. That causes vulnerability in all kinds of ways. A friend of mine reports hearing of a young man who was crawling across a room on his hands and knees looking for tiny bits of heroin to scrape up. He came up against a full-length mirror and saw himself, and thought, 'What are you doing with your life?'

So the person with the addiction problem may be at the lowest point he or she can reach before they ask for help. The next step may well be upwards, if the substance-dependent person can find his way to the help needed. The alternative is downwards to total catastrophe. The pastor may be one of a number of people that addicted sufferers reach out to in order to look for some hope and practical help, or at least sympathetic understanding of their situation.

Friends and family

All the people the addicted person is involved with, most importantly children and partners, but also other family members, colleagues and friends, are at risk to some extent. It is important for clergy to recognize this 'systemic' aspect of the phenomenon of addiction – it may well not only be the sufferer who needs help; others will be involved who may suffer the consequences of the addiction – personal, financial and so on. There is also the possibility of domestic violence. Where violence is known to be a factor, we may find ourselves in a position of working in close cooperation with the statutory services – doctors, social workers, even the police – particularly if the well-being of children is involved. In such situations issues of confidentiality will need to be considered, and at this point we will definitely need to be in contact with church safeguarding officers. Failure to follow proper procedure can lead to problems later on. In all our dealings with those affected by a person's addiction, we need to keep dated and reasonably detailed records of what *may* become legal evidence, including every conversation. Fortunately many churches have excellent and well-trained people who offer help and advice, such as formally employed diocesan safeguarding officers. It is vital to let them know about any difficult, abusive or even actively violent situations that we are involved in, not least for our own guidance and protection.

The pastor

The pastor is at risk by the very nature of the openness of the vicarage or clergy home to all who wish to visit, whether they are known to the pastor or not. Those who come to talk to us may have had no previous or recent contact with any particular church. We always answer the door, and visitors come for a variety of reasons, of which we will often be unaware at the first point of contact. It may be anything from arranging a wedding or a baptism to searching for spiritual guidance, or seeking help in a personal or family crisis.

It is natural that we want to help in whatever way is open to us; we regard responding to these situations as part of our vocation. Like Jesus himself, we find it objectionable to think of turning someone away when they are so much in need of whatever help they can find. Sadly, however, we have to recognize that in reality this attitude, although entirely praiseworthy, may not always be the best policy, particularly when we consider whether or not to let a stranger into our home.

We may perhaps know of clergy who have suffered as a result of admitting unknown people to the vicarage. This may be no worse than the theft of a relatively small amount of money or other items from the study; but on a number of occasions it has been the prelude to actual violence, including in the Diocese of Southwark where I live.

There is a risk to us and to anyone else who lives in the vicarage, especially our partners and children. We need to think clearly and sensibly about the people we let in, particularly if we don't know them and there is no one else in the house to give help if it is needed, and develop for ourselves some ground rules about our security. The Diocese of Southwark, for example, has produced a book on safeguarding – which I am pleased to say includes taking very seriously *the safety of the pastor*. All dioceses should have something similar to offer their clergy and other pastors. Diocesan safeguarding officers run good training courses, and many churches now require clergy and other authorized ministers and lay pastors to attend them from time to time.

Simple guidelines include avoiding handing out money at the vicarage door. Giving money can seem like a way of dealing with a problem quickly and easily, but will probably lead to further demands.

Experience is invaluable in helping us to make a quick assessment of what the visitor is really looking for. Of course, they will have a story to tell, which may or may not be 'true' in a literal sense. 'The better the tale, the bigger the rogue' was the litmus test applied by a former colleague of mine. Realistic? Cynical? Either way, it probably saved him from being 'taken in' unnecessarily on a number of occasions.

A long tale that alludes to personal, spiritual or relationship problems may well be the way in to a request for financial help, and our personal security depends a great deal on developing the ability to sort out what the real request is for. It is often hard to refuse a request for money without appearing to reject the person making it, even when we know that to be the best course of action.

The key is that in reality we can't always help everyone who comes to us, and there is nothing wrong in admitting that. It doesn't mean we have 'failed'. However, there may be opportunities to get to know someone we have met through the access provided by church or vicarage; this may lead to positive help being given to someone with an alcohol or drug misuse history, perhaps helping that person to get proper professional help.

A current picture of addiction and its impact

How many adults in the UK could be said to have a significant problem in relation to alcohol or drugs? The following diagram gives a helpful breakdown of recent statistics on dependent drinking.[2]

Most of the adult population of the UK are either non-drinkers (12%) or low-risk drinkers (67.1%) who drink within the Department of Health's guidelines (which are frequently revised) and suffer no harmful effects. These people are not considered *alcohol misusers*.

---

2 Dr David Ball, Institute of Psychiatry in London, unpublished lecture notes.

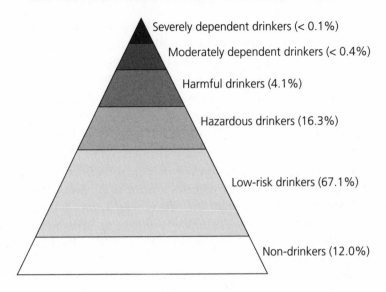

Severely dependent drinkers (< 0.1%)

Moderately dependent drinkers (< 0.4%)

Harmful drinkers (4.1%)

Hazardous drinkers (16.3%)

Low-risk drinkers (67.1%)

Non-drinkers (12.0%)

In his book *Theory of Addiction* (2006) Robert West gives an estimate of some common forms of illicit drug use in the UK, as shown in the table below.[3] It should be noted, however, that these figures depend entirely on *self-reported use* of the relevant drugs; the actual figures could well be significantly higher, as could the monthly costs.

Drug	% of population who are ever users	Use in past month %	% of ever users who have used in last month	Approximate monthly cost of regular use (£)
Cannabis	8.0	2.5	31	85
Amphetamine	4.0	0.3	7.5	100
Cocaine	2.0	0.4	20	160
Crack	0.3	0.1	33	450
Heroin	0.3	0.1	33	450
Ecstasy	2.0	0.4	20	40

---

3 West, *Theory of Addiction*, p. 28.

The financial aspect has a great impact, of course. It is not difficult for a heroin misuser to spend well in excess of £1,000 a week on the drug, as numerous television programmes, both factual and fictional, make clear. So the money has to come from somewhere, and often it is from such sources as burglary and street crime. It is likely that much, if not most, violent crime these days is drug related, even setting aside the institutionalized and sometimes extreme violence that is the hallmark of drug cartels, particularly in parts of Latin America.[4] Society as a whole pays a heavy price for addictive behaviour.

Equally, if a large amount of money is being spent on drugs, clearly it is not being spent on the family, on food, clothes, education, and ordinary kinds of entertainment and recreation. Addiction therefore undermines social functioning in a number of potentially disastrous ways. All of this can result in theft or violence within a family, and put the partner and children of the addicted person at risk of physical assault. The person who has the responsibility for keeping the family together will be put under enormous strain, and his or her physical or emotional health may well be compromised after a time.

When offering pastoral care to individuals, we need to think 'systemically' – about the various overlapping social systems that form the person's domestic environment and their place in the community.

The aspirational model and its application

I have referred earlier in this book to the specific intervention to addiction that I call my 'aspirational' model. It is now time to outline this approach in detail.

In my experience this model has undoubtedly proved its value, but it may not be suitable to use with everyone suffering with an addiction. Some of those we encounter are so badly damaged – temporarily or permanently – by drug misuse that they may not have the resources to respond to this

4 Roberto Saviano's book *Zero Zero Zero* explores this in detail.

approach at the point when we first meet them. But even in these cases, a time may come when the kind of conversation I am recommending can be an important factor. So it should be kept in mind for use when that becomes more possible. I mention this because it is so important that pastors should not feel bewildered or demoralized if we can't always provide help immediately, when we know we have much to offer. Ken Leech's 'mysterious element' in drug addiction is undoubtedly a factor here.

The beginning

My aspirational model was not a planned or thought-out intervention; it suggested itself to me during an informal meeting with a young man who was in treatment for addiction. If anything, *it came from the user himself.* He was expressing deep frustrations about the treatment he was receiving. It was not that he felt that the professional people trying to help him were not good at their job. But he wanted to make a significant breakthrough that would free him from his substance dependency. And nothing in the treatment was helping him to make that radical change of perspective. It was a form of treatment that aimed to help him understand better why he had gradually become so powerless to give up the drugs for himself. That can be an important thing to achieve, but more was needed.

In our conversation at the rehab centre where he was living, I felt his frustration very strongly. And it was in that frame of mind that I suddenly posed to him the (as I see it now) all-important question: *What do you want out of life?*

Although he wasn't able to come up with a definite answer on the spot, my question made quite an impact on him. I discovered this quite a long time afterwards, when he was clearly very much better. In fact he told me that the question had enabled him to begin the most important part of his recovery, which I am happy to say has been very successful: he now lives in his own flat, has a supportive family and good friends, and has been for several years running a successful business.

Goals and desires

So the vital task for us is to try to understand how this question about goals and desires for living helped him (and others) to change so dramatically. There are several factors here.

- First, my approach was one that treated him as a *person* rather than a *problem*. It is very easy with medical conditions to focus initially on the illness, disease or disability rather than on the person. We may respond to seeing a visually impaired person with a white stick by offering to help him across a busy road. There is nothing at all wrong with that wish to assist. But there is perhaps a danger of seeing the obvious physical need and responding to it without really regarding the recipient of our good deed as a person. And with addiction, perhaps because of the confusion and chaos that can arise out of substance dependency (or dependency on gambling or shopping, for example), we can fall into the trap of seeing the problem rather than the person. In fact, I normally avoid using the word 'problem' at all – and quite deliberately.

- Second, I regard the use of my question about goals for living – however we may phrase it – as a *positive* response to the person. It is based on the question that Jesus put to the blind man Bartimaeus: 'What do you want me to do for you?'[5] People who are substance dependent often feel despondent about ever being able to give up their destructive habit; this can be demoralizing, thus setting up a negative feedback loop that in turn feeds the habit. Family or friends may try to help at times, but in doing so no doubt unintentionally reinforce that undermining process, rather than giving the person some much needed positive encouragement and psychological reinforcement. My approach provides an antidote to those negative experiences.

---

5 See Mark 10.46–52.

- Third, my question offers an approach to treatment that focuses not on what the person is trying to recover *from* but on what he or she is recovering *for*. It points towards the possibility of a better future, without the drug. As an American friend of mine expressed it recently in an email, 'Recovery that is not better than the addiction is fragile.'

A *positive approach*

We should remember that the way we approach an addicted person may well help to open up a conversation about what is going on in her life apart from the addiction. There may be some history of anxiety or depression that has not been attended to, or relationship difficulties. She may have been under excessive or unreasonable pressure at work and not felt able to discuss these issues with anyone. Any underlying problem such as depression will almost certainly have contributed to the misuse of a drug, or alcohol dependency. As these factors emerge in our pastoral work we can begin to look at them and find helpful ways of addressing them: we will probably have something of importance to contribute ourselves. We should naturally be aware of our own boundaries and limitations, not least in knowing when it is appropriate to look for other forms of professional help, perhaps through medical intervention, counselling or psychotherapy. But the way in which we approach the person at the outset will generate an environment in which that individual will begin to trust us because we have this positive approach to her.

My initial question about personal goals, longings, desires and aspirations has, I believe, much to offer because it is fundamentally a positive approach. It puts the person receiving help at the centre of the picture and concentrates its attention on the person rather than the 'problem'. We may believe that trying to identify the reasons for an addiction is important – but if we begin here we may find that we add to the person's frustration rather than helping him to look at the situation in a radically new and more promising way. Some treatments seem to encourage the addicted person to feel ashamed of his past behaviour under the influence of drugs, but I do not believe such an approach to be generally helpful.

Setting people free

My aspirational approach is founded to a great extent on Augustine's pursuit of the *summum bonum* – the quest for the greatest good. It also provides a pragmatic pastoral and clinical programme that looks at the *positive longings and aspirations of the individual*. I believe that the two can be used together to bring freedom and hope to the person who is imprisoned by the misuse of a drug.

The young man I mentioned earlier had been viewed by many people, including his family and the people involved in his rehabilitation, as a *problem*. He had been made to feel guilty at times for being enslaved to alcohol and its consequences – which is very strange indeed if we truly believe that addiction not only exists but should be regarded as a disease. That is not to remove all the responsibility for improving that person's situation from him, any more than would be the case if he was suffering from heart problems, diabetes or cancer. We all need to take some responsibility for getting the right kind of help when it is needed. What I was doing with my question to the young man was addressing issues that I suspect no one had discussed with him before, offering a positive approach that focused on what he would like to make of his life, rather than being overly concerned with the past which had been so difficult and painful for him. This approach was undoubtedly much more successful. I am convinced that those who have pastoral contact with people who misuse substances can use this technique; in essence it is very simple, but it can be a potential game-changer.

God, grace and the welcome of the Church

At a profoundly theological level this resonates well with the theology of Augustine. By making God the absolute centre of all desire, we are able to construct a hierarchy of lesser desires in such a way that they do not distract us from the ultimate goal of human life, which is to be in relationship with God, both in this life and beyond it. If there seems to be a rather negative or uncompromising element to this, it may be helpful to recognize that Augustine's intention is to encourage people to see the benefits of making God the centre of our lives, a process that for him involved years of interior struggle and conflict. He firmly believed, as he became more and deeply committed to this view, that there are ultimate and penultimate goals for human living, and that the lesser goals can impede our journey to what is of supreme value. It is a way of life that probably never finds complete fulfilment in this world, but it is a journey that we are all invited to undertake.

In our pastoral and spiritual work with others this is something we should invest in: in the case of the substance-dependent person it is a way of looking at life that may well help to set new goals for people who have lost their way and need to be brought back to a vision of life that is positive, healthy and life-affirming, in terms of both their physical, emotional and spiritual health, and their human relationships. The way we do this will need to be tailored to some extent to the individual we are trying to help (and the recognition that not all those who are aware that they have a spiritual need will necessarily find that need met in our church services).

I am reminded in saying this of the important healing potential of *grace* – as discussed earlier in the work of Gerald May. Grace can be offered to the addiction sufferer through channels such as the contribution of the confident and professional Christian pastor, but the value of this will be greatly enhanced, as May points out, when people can be welcomed into the worshipping life of a Christian congregation. This is absolutely correct, but it is not always easy to achieve. Congregations need to be well informed about the nature of addiction; there can be prejudice in some churches about addiction and marginalization of people facing a range of psychological or emotional difficulties. These attitudes are often the result of ignorance or fear, which is why we need to teach our congregations about mental and emotional disorders, including addictions. Enabling congregations to be truly welcoming to all who enter through the church door is not always an easy matter, and it again raises questions about safeguarding – of both the person with the addiction and the whole community. But with good and sensitively offered education all congregations can be better equipped to welcome all people confidently. I hope that this book will be helpful in this regard.

This approach resonates very strongly with the founding principles of organizations like AA, who emphasize in the quest for wholeness and healing the importance of recognizing the benefits that come from seeing God, or our Higher Power, as a vital source of recovery from substance dependency. The Twelve Step programme for recovery devised by AA is set out in full on page 90.

Concluding Reflections

The aim of this book is to assist people who are involved in pastoral ministry. Some of the ideas presented here (such as Osmer's four-stage description of pastoral care) may be useful in general terms, across the board of our work as Christian pastors. But my particular concern here has been to offer help and guidance to ministers offering pastoral care to people whose lives have been adversely affected by the misuse of alcohol and drugs – both illicit, non-prescription drugs such as cocaine, and prescription drugs such as painkillers[1].

In this book I have included information about how drugs work in the neurological system, and how this can set up a physiological dependence. I have raised questions about whether addiction is best thought of as a disease, and concluded that it should be, which also raises theological questions about personal responsibility and sinfulness. It also questions (based on Leech's work) the assumption that addicted people require some specific form of ministry that is different from the ministry that we might offer to others who are not substance dependent. I have argued the theory that because so many treatment plans seem either to fail completely or only work for a limited period of time, there is an urgent need for a new model of treatment, particularly in terms of psychological intervention. And one very important point is the recognition that when a member of a family has a drug addiction, it is often the whole family that suffers as a result.

---

1 Damian Thompson devotes some space in his book *The Fix* to the increasing phenomenon of the misuse of prescription drugs in many parts of the world.

I avoid using the word 'problem' when discussing people with addictions, on the basis that if addiction is a form of disease (however we define this word) then it makes no more sense to describe addiction as a problem than to so describe any other disease: the word 'problem' in this context can be a form of negative discrimination. I also think there is much to be gained by looking at the suggestion of modern psychology that our human personalities are many-faceted and change over time – and this may help to explain why some people genuinely desire to give up using drugs and yet go on using them, which is evidence of internal conflict.

From this discussion and from my personal experience of time spent with people with addictions, I suggest that although we may at some stage need to think about why an individual has become substance dependent, the most important issues to discuss relate to the person's desires, longings, hopes and personal aspirations, so that their drug misuse can be understood in relation to that context rather than looked at in isolation. So it may well be more helpful to address questions like 'What are you recovering *for?*' rather than 'What are you trying to recover *from?*'

I have included ideas about sources of help available for our work in the addiction ministry. It is not easy to be specific about the advice offered in local situations, not least because, in the UK at least, the way in which the provision of drug misuse clinical care is structured seems to change frequently, as do the contact details of relevant organizations. The internet is a highly useful resource for finding locally based professional help, whether directly for an addicted individual, or for advice for their families or perhaps for ourselves in our pastoral work.

It is of great importance that we pay attention to our own personal well-being and safety and that of our families. This is likely to involve some discrimination about who we let into our homes, no matter how needy a person may seem to be. When I was a hospital chaplain I always insisted that the first duty of my team was to take proper care of themselves, because we can't care for others properly if we can't look after ourselves.

And it is always worth remembering that we have not failed if an addicted person relapses: sadly, we have to recognize that this often happens, and sometimes we may make only a limited – though valuable – contribution to an individual's recovery. Medical practitioners in the addictions field experience the same thing, but continue the work in the hope that those they care for will eventually get better.

Often it will be helpful in our work to encourage people to seek help themselves through organizations such as AA or NA. The first step on that journey – and usually the hardest step – is to try to move the individual concerned towards an acceptance that he needs help, as so many find that a long and difficult or even frightening journey. But as we develop a trustful relationship with such people this process can sometimes begin, as they develop the belief that we will endeavour to help and support them through recovery for as long as that may take.

I have offered some possible explanations of the causes of substance dependency, including the observation, derived from the world of biogenetic science, that there is almost certainly a genetic element in the path to some addictive behaviours. In my own experience I have seen that alcoholism, for example, can affect people in several generations of families. But there have to be other factors, and these often relate to day-to-day difficulties, perhaps because of depression or anxiety or emotionally distressing circumstances such as bereavement. Equally, we must beware of overgeneralizing. There may be as many causes of addiction as there are addicted people.

I have also suggested a way of assessing whether a person we are concerned about is in fact truly addicted, whether to alcohol or to a prescribed or illicit drug.[2] Many drinkers of alcohol are not truly dependent on it, though long-term excessive intake *may* be suggestive of alcoholism, and a similar argument can be used about drug users.

---

2 See the helpful symptom checklist created by Griffith Edwards on page xxiv of *Matters of Substance*.

And I have presented Richard Osmer's four-point methodology that addresses pastoral ministry in general, in the belief that this can be adapted to cover a number of pastoral needs, including substance dependency. This is a highly useful pragmatic approach, based on his long experience of working as a Christian pastor and on theologically based reflections on that experience.

In terms of the best pastoral approach to many addicted people, I have presented my aspirational model, which arose out of a particular conversation but also led me to see the relevance of Augustine's insistence that human life is most fulfilled when its primary focus is God. If our hearts are truly restless until they rest in God, then surely it makes sense to see the use of drugs and alcohol, and other consumable commodities, as secondary to the pursuit of spiritual goals in our lives. And in this context, the question *What are you looking for in life?* addresses this pursuit, and can lead to big changes in the behaviour of an addicted person. That is not to say that the question will lead instantaneously to a conversation about spiritual matters. But even a less ambitious project, if it results in the recognition and establishment of some more ordinary aims and objectives, is a step in that direction.

I believe that the model of pastoral care I am recommending here is one that can be utilized not only in pastoral ministry but also beyond the boundaries of religious and spiritual forms of care and ministry in the work of clinicians specializing in the addictions field of medicine. It would be good to see more conversations about the care of addicted people taking place in many community situations, perhaps in local doctors' surgeries, hospitals and clinics. In the mutuality of shared experience there is always hope for change for the better.

Community Resources for Working with Addicted People

What resources are available in the communities where we live and work to help us in our offering of good pastoral care to those who are substance dependent?

Without wanting to sound alarm bells unnecessarily, it is worth making the point that emergencies do happen; if it is suspected that someone has taken an overdose of any substance, an emergency call should be made *immediately* so that a potentially dangerous or life-threatening situation can be dealt with quickly and professionally.

Any list of professional resources should include the **local doctors' surgery** and the names of general practitioners (GPs). Obviously that requires a degree of awareness and honesty on the part of the sufferer in order to make that appointment, as we don't usually go to the doctor unless we know and accept that we need to. And we have to be realistic: in the UK the average consultation between doctor and patient lasts about ten minutes, far too short a time to deal with the complex aspects of addiction and their impact, not only on the patient, but on whole families. But doctors may have experts in their clinic or surgery team, or should know where to get additional help from established community drug outreach teams.

A number of well-known organizations deal with specific needs, for example **Alcoholics Anonymous**. They provide what is in effect a network of self-help groups, which have no medical or clinical input and no therapist. It all depends on the willingness of individual members of the groups to be open and honest with one another about their needs, and to be mutually supportive and non-judgemental. *It is vital to know that these groups behave on the basis of strict and absolute confidentiality.* They make use of the Twelve Step programme, which is worth setting out here as it is used in groups all over the world. It is firmly based on spiritual (though non-denominational) principles; there is also now a secular form of the Steps. In its original AA format these are the Steps towards recovery from alcohol addiction:

1 We admitted we were powerless over alcohol – that our lives had become unmanageable.
2 We came to believe that a Power greater than ourselves could restore us to sanity.
3 We made a decision to turn our will and our lives over to the care of God as we understood him.
4 We made a searching and fearless moral inventory of ourselves.
5 We admitted to God, to ourselves, and to another human being the exact nature of our wrongs.
6 We were entirely ready to have God remove all those defects of character.
7 We humbly asked God to remove our shortcomings.
8 We made a list of all persons we had harmed, and became willing to make amends to them all.
9 We made direct amends to such people wherever possible, except when to do so would injure them or others.
10 We continued to take personal inventory, and when we were wrong, promptly admitted it.
11 We sought through prayer and meditation to improve our conscious contact with God, as we understood him, praying only for knowledge of his will for us and the power to carry that out.
12 Having had a spiritual awakening as the result of these steps, we tried to carry this message to alcoholics, and to practise these principles in all our affairs.

The Steps form a programme that is the basis of the work done in AA groups, helping people to engage with the process of recovery. It is believed by many in AA, however, that the process of recovery is a lifelong undertaking – the idea being that in this way of looking at alcoholism there is really no such person as an 'ex-alcoholic'. The **Drinkaware** website also has helpful information.

For the families of people with alcohol dependency the related organization **Al-Anon** is an important resource. It is not just the drug or alcohol user who may need help, but other family members as well.

For the users of non-prescription drugs such as cannabis, spice, heroin or crack cocaine, there is a similar organization: **Narcotics Anonymous;** and **Cocaine Anonymous** works in a similar way.

All these organizations can be found online, including details of local branches.

www.talktofrank.com is a service directed particularly at young people who need to ask important questions about the effects of drugs, and what confidential help is available if they are getting into difficulties but find it hard to talk about them with family, teachers or friends. Information and contact details are on the website.

For those with a professional interest in the subject, including pastors, there is a useful resource called **Change, Grow, Live,** which has the advantage of providing information about local clinics that specialize in the treatment of addicted people all over the UK. Other countries may well have similar websites.

Christian pastors may find suitable **training programmes** associated with particular areas or Anglican dioceses. I have led courses in the dioceses of Southwark, London and Guildford. It is worth looking out for any training programmes that are provided as part of your regular ministerial in-service training provision. *It can be very helpful to discuss situations you have been involved in with others who are doing similar* *pastoral work.* And the person leading the training should be well versed in the psychological and theological issues, offering relevant and up-to-date information about what other help is available on a local basis. If there is no such course where you are, you could suggest it to the people in charge of ministerial training, particularly if you have had direct involvement in difficult or challenging situations in your own ministry. At times we all need support in our work, and in the case of addiction this is particularly important, so conversations with colleagues and other experienced and sympathetic clergy will be very important to us as we try to offer our help. We do not have to work in isolation.

Many of the books listed in the **Bibliography** are likely to be helpful, especially those referred to in the text. Kenneth Leech's *Drugs and Pastoral Care* is one that I return to often. It is in some ways controversial, taking a fairly relaxed view of the drug scene, but its emphasis on an egalitarian approach to pastoral care and its refusal to ignore the highly mysterious element in ministry to addicted people are important issues that he discusses with honesty and sensitivity. There is also a sense in Leech's theoretical model, and his experience of working pastorally and spiritually with addicted people over many years, that he does not try to rush things. He is aware that the process of caring for people who use or misuse drugs can take a long time, and may need to be repeated more than once. This approach works somewhat against the grain of current clinical practice in which quick results are viewed as cost-effective and are therefore highly desirable. In his pastoral work Leech demonstrates on the basis of long experience a willingness to allow the 'client' to be in control and to set the agenda. Imposing a set of values on the situation may reflect the ideas and views of the pastor more than the genuine needs of the person receiving care. Sometimes, in pastoral work of all kinds, we need to divest ourselves of power.

Bibliography

Adams, Tony and Ian Ridley, *Addicted*. London: Collins Willow, 1999.

Alcoholics Anonymous, *The Story of How Many Thousands of Men and Women Have Recovered from Alcoholism*, 3rd edn. New York: AA World Services, 1976 (known as the 'Big Book').

Allan, David G. C., *Science, Philanthropy and Religion in 18th Century Teddington: Stephen Hales DD, FRS 1677–1761*. Twickenham: Borough of Twickenham Local History Society, 2004.

Augustine, *Confessions*, trans. Henry Chadwick. Oxford: World's Classics, 1992.

Augustine, *De Doctrina Christiana*, trans. Edmund Hill OP ('Teaching Christianity'). New York: New City Press, 1996.

Augustine, *Lectures or Tractates on the Gospel According to St John*, trans. Marcus B. Dick. *The Oxford Group & Alcoholics Anonymous*. Kihei, HI: Paradise Research Publications, 1998.

Ball, David, 'Addiction science and its genetics', *Addiction* 103 (2007): 360–7.

Barnard, Marina, *Drug Addiction and Families*. London: Jessica Kingsley, 2007.

Barrett, C. K., *Paul: An Introduction to His Thought*. London, Geoffrey Chapman, 1978.

Bepko, Claudia (ed.), *Feminism and Addiction*. London: Haworth Press, 1991.

Blakebrough, Eric, *No Quick Fix*. Basingstoke: Marshall Pickering, 1986.

Boon, Marcus, *The Road of Excess*. Cambridge, MA: Harvard University Press, 2002.

Booth, Leo, *Spirituality and Recovery*, 4th edn. Deerfield Beach, FL: Health Communications, 2012.

Bretherton, Luke, *The Use and Abuse of Drugs*. Cambridge: Grove Books, 2004.

Brett, Mary, 'Ten key facts that teachers need to know about cannabis', *Education and Health* 26:3 (2008): 47–9.

Briers, Stephen, *Brilliant Cognitive Behavioural Therapy*. Harlow: Pearson Education, 2009.

Brown, Peter, *Augustine of Hippo: A Biography*. Columbia University Press, 1988. New edn, London: Faber, 2000.

Bunch, David and Angus Ritchie (eds), *Prayer and Prophecy: The Essential Kenneth Leech*. London: Darton, Longman and Todd, 2009.

Cabinet Office (UK) Report, *Alcohol Misuse: How Much Does It Cost?* (2003).

Chadwick, Henry, *Augustine*. Oxford: Oxford University Press, 1986.

Clinebell, Howard, *Understanding and Counseling Persons with Alcohol, Drug and Behavioral Addictions*. Nashville, TN: Abingdon Press, 1998.

Coakley, Sarah (ed.), *Faith, Rationality and the Passions*. Chichester: Wiley-Blackwell, 2012.

Colvin, Rod, *Prescription Drug Addiction, the Hidden Epidemic*. Omaha, Nebraska: Addicus Books, 2012.

Cook, Christopher C. H., *Alcohol, Addiction and Christian Ethics*. Cambridge: Cambridge University Press, 2006.

Cook, Christopher C. H., *The Philokalia and the Inner Life: On Passions and Prayer*. Cambridge: James Clarke, 2011.

Cook, Christopher C. H., *The Use and Misuse of Alcohol*. Cambridge: Grove Books, 2007.

Copleston, F. C., *Aquinas*. Harmondsworth: Penguin, 1967.

Cranfield, C. E. B., *Romans: A Shorter Commentary*. Edinburgh: T. and T. Clark, 1995.

Davies, John Booth, *The Myth of Addiction: An Application of the Psychological Theory of Attribution to Illicit Drug Use*, 2nd edn. Philadelphia, PA: Harwood Academic Publishers, 1992.

Diocese of London, *Knocking at Heaven's Door: Challenges and opportunities presented by the Casual Caller in the Parish*, 1996.

Diocese of Southwark, *The Safety of Clergy at Work: Report of Working Party*, 1998.

Dodd, C. H., *The Epistle of Paul to the Romans*. London: Fontana, 1959.

Dunn, J. G. D., *Romans 1–8*. Dallas, TX: Word Biblical Commentaries, 1988.

Dunn, J. G. D., *The Theology of Paul the Apostle*. Edinburgh: T. and T. Clark, 1998.

Edwards, Griffith, *Matters of Substance: Drugs: Is Legalization the Right Answer – or the Wrong Question?* London: Penguin, 2005.

Edwards, Griffith, E. Jane Marshall and Christopher C. H. Cook, *The Treatment of Drinking Problems: A Guide for the Helping Professions*, 3rd edn. Cambridge: Cambridge University Press, 1997.

Fingarette, H., in Ruth C. Engs (ed.), *Controversies in the Addiction's Field*, Volume 1. Dubuque, IA: Kendall/Hunt, 1990.

Ford, David F., *Christian Wisdom, Desiring God and Learning in Love*. Cambridge: Cambridge University Press, 2007.

Ford, David F., *The Future of Christian Theology*. Oxford: Wiley-Blackwell, 2011.

Furnish, V. P., *The Love Command in the New Testament*. London: SCM Press, 1972.

Gill, A. A., *Pour Me: A Life*. London: Weidenfeld and Nicolson, 2016.

Glenny, Misha, *McMafia*. London: Vintage Books, 2009.

Gorringe, T. J., *The Education of Desire*. Harrisburg, PA: Trinity Press International, 2001.

Hales, Stephen, *A friendly admonition to the drinkers of gin, brandy, and other distilled spirituous liquors*, 6th edn, with additions. London: SPCK, 1800.

Hewitt, Jim, *Alcoholism: A Matter of Choice*. Rochester, VT: Schenkman, 1999.

Higgs, John, *I Have America Surrounded: The Life of Timothy Leary*. Fort Lee, NJ: Barricade Books, 2006.

James, Erica, *The Holiday*. London: Orion, 2000.

Jason-Lloyd, Leonard, *Misuse of Drugs*. Bristol: Jordan, 2009.

Jellinek, E. M., *The Disease Concept of Alcoholism*. New Brunswick, NJ: Hillhouse Press, 1960.

Kerouac, Jack, *On the Road*. London: Penguin, 2000.

Leech, Kenneth, *Drugs and Pastoral Care*. London: Darton, Longman and Todd, 1998.

Leech, Kenneth, 'Drugs and the Church', General Synod Miscellaneous Paper 527, 1998.

Leech, Kenneth, *Pastoral Care and the Drug Scene*. London: SPCK, 1970.

Lockley, Paul, *Counselling Heroin and other Drug Users*. London: Free Association Books, 1995.

Luther, Martin, *Table Talk*. London: H. G. Bohn, 1857.

May, Gerald, *Addiction and Grace*. San Francisco, CA: Harper Collins, 1991.

McFarland, Ian A., *In Adam's Fall: A Meditation on the Christian Doctrine of Original Sin*. Oxford: Wiley-Blackwell, 2010.

Meilaender, Gilbert, 'Sweet necessities: Food, sex and Saint Augustine', *Journal of Religious Ethics* 29:1 (2001): 3–18.

Mercadante, Linda A., *Victims and Sinners: Spiritual Roots of Addiction and Recovery*. Louisville, KY: Westminster John Knox Press, 1996.

Miles, Margaret R., *Desire and Delight: A New Reading of Augustine's Confessions*. Eugene, OR: Wipf and Stock, 2006.

Moore, Sebastian, *Jesus the Liberator of Desire*. New York: Crossroad, 1989.

Nakken, Craig, *The Addictive Personality: Understanding the Addictive Process and Compulsive Behavior*, 2nd edn. Center City, MN: Hazelden Press, 1996.

Nelson, James B., *Thirst: God and the Alcoholic Experience*. Louisville, KY: Westminster John Knox Press, 2004.

Nicholls, James, *The Politics of Alcohol: A History of the Drink Question in England*. Manchester: Manchester University Press, 2009.

Nutt, David J. (et al.), 'Drug harm in the UK: A multi criteria decision analysis', *The Lancet* 37:6 (2010): 11ff.

Orford, Jim, *Excessive Appetites: A Psychological View of Addictions*, 2nd edn. Chichester: Wiley, 2001.

Osmer, Richard, *Practical Theology*. Grand Rapids, MI: Eerdmans, 2008.

Plomin, Robert, *Behavioral Genetics*, 4th edn. New York: Worth Publishers, 2001.

Polkinghorne, John and Michael Welker, *Faith in the Living God*. London: SPCK, 2001.

Radmall, Bill, *Insight into Addiction*. Farnham: CWR, 2009.

Rycroft, Charles, *A Critical Dictionary of Psychoanalysis*. London: Nelson, 1968.

Saviano, Roberto, *Zero Zero Zero*. London: Penguin, 2013.

Seligman, Martin E. P., *Authentic Happiness*. New York: Free Press, 2002.

Smith, Kelly, *Footballer: My Story*. London: Bantam, 2012.

Stendahl, Krister, *Paul among Jews and Gentiles, and Other Essays*. Philadelphia, PA: Fortress Press, 1976.

Stump, E., and N. Kretzmann, *The Cambridge Companion to Augustine*. Cambridge: Cambridge University Press, 2002.

Thayil, Jeet, *Narcopolis*. London: Faber, 2012.

Theissen, G., *Psychological Aspects of Pauline Theology*. Edinburgh: T. and T. Clark, 1987.

Thomas Aquinas, *Summa Theologica*, Part II, English translation. London: Burns, Oates & Washbourne, 1922.

Thompson, Damian, *The Fix*. London: Collins, 2012.

Tillich, Paul, *Systematic Theology*, Volume 2. London: James Nisbet and Sons, 1957.

Turner, Léon, *Theology, Psychology and the Plural Self*. Farnham: Ashgate, 2008.

Valverde, Mariana, *Diseases of the Will: Alcohol and the Dilemmas of Freedom*, Cambridge Studies in Law and Society. Cambridge: Cambridge University Press, 1998.

Watts, Fraser N., *Theology and Psychology*. Aldershot: Ashgate, 2002.

Watts, Fraser N., Rebecca Nye and Sara B. Savage, *Psychology for Christian Ministry*. London: Routledge, 2002.

Webber, M., *Steps of Transformation: An Orthodox Priest Explores the Twelve Steps*. Ben Lomond: Conciliar Press, 2003.

West, Robert, *Theory of Addiction*. Oxford: Blackwell, 2006.

Williams, Rowan, 'Language, reality and desire in Augustine's De Doctrina', *Journal of Literature and Theology* 3:2 (1989): 138–50.

Williams, Rowan, *On Augustine*. London: Bloomsbury, 2016.

Ziesler, J., *Paul's Letter to the Romans*. London: SCM Press, 1989.